Rosie the Riveter and Women's Roles During World War II

SB Jeffrey

The role of the book within our culture is changing. The change is brought on by new ways to acquire & use content, the rapid dissemination of information and real-time peer collaboration on a global scale. Despite these changes one thing is clear--"the book" in it's traditional form continues to play an important role in learning and communication. The book you are holding in your hands utilizes the unique characteristics of the Internet -- relying on web infrastructure and collaborative tools to share and use resources in keeping with the characteristics of the medium (user-created, defying control, etc.)--while maintaining all the convenience and utility of a real book.

Contents

Articles

Women in The World Wars   1
Women's roles in the World Wars   1

The Greatest Generation   10
Greatest Generation   10

The Home Front   13
United States home front during World War II   13

Women in The Workforce   33
Women in the workforce   33

Rosie   53
Rosie the Riveter   53
Willow Run Airport   59
Richmond Shipyards   62
Rosie the Riveter/World War II Home Front National Historical Park   64
The Life and Times of Rosie the Riveter   74

W.A.S.P.   76
Women Airforce Service Pilots   76

The U.S.O.   87
United Service Organizations   87

Red Cross   99
International Red Cross and Red Crescent Movement   99

Women's Land Army   **124**
    Woman's Land Army of America   124

References
    Article Sources and Contributors   126
    Image Sources, Licenses and Contributors   127

Women in The World Wars

Women's roles in the World Wars

There is little doubt that **women's work in the two World Wars** of the twentieth century was an important factor in the outcome of both wars. This involvement changed the social status and working lives of women in many countries from that point onwards.

Women's contribution to both wars was significant; though the attitudes towards their contribution were typically paternalistic.

Women's role prior to World War I

Prior to the First World War women's role in society in western countries was generally confined to the domestic sphere (but not necessarily their own home) and to certain types of jobs: 'Women's Work'. In Great Britain for example, just before World War I, out of an adult population of about 24 million women, around 1.7 million worked in domestic service,

Rosie the Riveter: "We Can Do It!" - Many women first found economic strength in World War II-era manufacturing jobs.

800,000 worked in the textile manufacturing industry, 600,000 worked in the clothing trades, 500,000 worked in commerce and 260,000 in local and national government (including teaching). The British textile and clothing trades, in particular, employed far more women than men and could be regarded as 'women's work'.

While some women managed to receive a tertiary education and others to go into non-traditional career paths, for the most part women were expected to be primarily involved in "duties at home" and "women's work". Before 1914, only a few countries (New Zealand, Australia, and several Scandinavian nations) had given the right to vote to women (see Women's suffrage), and apart from these countries women were little involved in the political process.

More than any previous wars, World Wars I and II hinged as much on industrial production as they did on battlefield clashes. With millions of men away fighting and with the inevitable horrendous casualties, there was a severe shortage of labour in a range of industries, from rural and farm work to city office jobs.

During both World War I and World War II, women were called on, by necessity, to do work and to take on roles that were outside their traditional gender expectations. In Great Britain this was known as a process of "Dilution" and was strongly contested by the trade unions, particularly in the engineering and ship building industries. Women did, for the duration of both World Wars, take on jobs that were traditionally regarded as skilled "men's work". However, in accordance with the agreement negotiated with the trade unions, women undertaking jobs covered by the Dilution agreement lost their jobs at the end of the First World War.

World War I

See also: Women in the First World War

Home front

By 1914 nearly 5.09 million out of the 23.8 million women in Britain were working. Thousands worked in munitions factories (see Canary girl), offices and large hangars used to build aircraft. Women were also involved in knitting socks for the soldiers on the front, as well as other voluntary work, but as a matter of survival women had to work for paid employment for the sake of their families. Many women worked as volunteers serving at the Red Cross, encouraged the sale of war bonds or planted "victory gardens".

The United States Navy began accepting women for enlisted service during World War I

Not only did women have to keep "the home fires burning" but they took on voluntary and paid employment that was diverse in scope and showed that women were highly capable in diverse fields of endeavor. There is little doubt that this expanded view of the role of women in society did change the outlook of what women could do and their place in the workforce. Although women were still paid less than men in the workforce, women's equality were starting to arise as women were now getting paid two-thirds of the typical pay for men. However, the extent of this change is open to historical debate. In part because of female participation in the war effort Canada, the USA, Great Britain, and a number of European countries extended suffrage to women in the years after the First World War.

Military service

Nursing became almost the only area of female contribution that involved being at the front and experiencing the war. In Britain the Queen Alexandra's Royal Army Nursing Corps, First Aid Nursing Yeomanry (FANY) and Voluntary Aid Detachment were all started before World War I. The VADs were not allowed in the front line until 1915.

The only belligerent to deploy female combat troops in substantial numbers was the Russian Provisional Government in 1917. Its few "Women's Battalions" fought well, but failed to provide the propaganda value expected of them and were disbanded before the end of the year. In the later Russian Civil War, the Bolsheviks would also employ women infantry.

World War II

See also: Home front during World War II

With this expanded horizon of opportunity and confidence, and with the extended skill base that many women could now give to paid and voluntary employment, women's roles in World War II were even more extensive than in the First World War. By 1945, more than 2.2 million women were working in the war industries, building ships, aircraft, vehicles, and weaponry. Women also worked in factories, munitions plants and farms, and also drove trucks, provided logistic support for soldiers and entered professional areas of work that were previously the preserve of men. In the Allied countries thousands of women enlisted as nurses serving on the front lines. Thousands of others joined defensive militias at home and there was a great increase in the number of women serving in the military itself, particularly in the Red Army (see below).

Several hundred thousand women served in combat roles, especially in anti-aircraft units. The U.S. decided not to use women in combat because public opinion would not tolerate it.

This necessity to use the skills and the time of women was heightened by the nature of the war itself. While World War I was mainly fought in France and was a war arguably without clear aggressor or villain, World War II involved global conflict on an unprecedented scale against certain aggressors. In these circumstances the absolute urgency of mobilizing the entire population made the expansion of the role of women inevitable. The hard skilled labour of women was symbolized in the United States by the figure of Rosie the Riveter.

Many women served in the resistances of France, Italy, and Poland, and in the British SOE which aided these.

Britain

In Britain, women were essential to the war effort, in both civilian and military roles. The contribution by civilian men and women to the British war effort was acknowledged with the use of the words "Home Front" to describe the battles that were being fought on a domestic level with rationing, recycling, and war work, such as in munitions factories and farms. Men were thus released into the military. Women were "drafted" in the sense that they were assigned jobs by the government, including non-combat jobs in the military, including the Women's Royal Naval Service (WRNS or "Wrens") and the Auxiliary Territorial Service (ATS). Auxiliary services such as the Air Transport Auxiliary also recruited women. British women were not drafted into combat units, but could volunteer for combat duty in anti-aircraft units, which shot down German planes and V-1 missiles. Civilian women joined the Special Operations Executive (SOE), which used them in high-danger roles as secret agents and underground radio operators in Nazi occupied Europe.

A woman machinist talking with Eleanor Roosevelt during her goodwill tour of Great Britain in 1942

Finland

Much like in the United Kingdom, the Finnish women took part in defence: nursing, air raid signaling, rationing and hospitalization of the wounded. Their organization was called Lotta Svärd, where voluntary women took part in auxiliary work of the armed forces to help those fighting on the front. Lotta Svärd was one of the largest, if not the largest, voluntary group in World War II. Though they never held guns (a rule among the Lottas), without women's help Finland probably could not have held off the Soviet forces as long as it did.

Germany

The Third Reich, contrary to popular belief, had similar roles for women. The SS-Helferinnen were regarded as part of the SS if they had undergone training at a Reichsschule SS but all other female workers were regarded as being contracted to the SS and chosen largely from concentration camps. Women also served in auxiliary units in the navy (Kriegshelferinnen), air force (Luftnachrichtenhelferinnen) and army (Nachrichtenhelferin). Hundreds of women auxiliaries (Aufseherin) served for the SS in the camps, the majority of which were at Ravensbrück. In Germany women also worked, and were told by Hitler to produce more pure Aryan children to fight in future wars.

Poland

In occupied Poland, as elsewhere, women played a major role in the resistance movement, putting them in the front line. Their most important role was as couriers carrying messages between cells of the resistance movement and distributing news broadsheets and operating clandestine printing presses. During partisan attacks on Nazi forces and installations they served as scouts.

A grave of three Polish female soldiers who fell during the Invasion of Poland, 1939, among their colleagues interred at Warsaw's Powązki Cemetery

During the Warsaw Rising of 1944, female members of the Home Army were couriers and medics, but many carried weapons and took part in the fighting. Among the more notable women of the Home Army was Wanda Gertz who created and commanded *DYSK* (Women's sabotage unit). For her bravery in these activities and later in the Warsaw Uprising she was awarded Poland's highest awards - Virtuti Militari and Polonia Restituta. One of the articles of the capitulation was that the German Army recognized them as full members of the armed forces and needed to set up separate Prisoner-of-war camps to hold over 2000 women prisoners-of-war.

Soviet Union

See also: Women in the Russian and Soviet military

United States of America

See also: United States home front during World War II

American women also saw combat during World War II, first as nurses in the Army Nurse Corps and United States Navy Nurse Corps during the Attack on Pearl Harbor on 7 December 1941, and the Japanese invasion of the Philippines. The Women's Army Auxiliary Corps, Women's Naval Reserve and United States Marine Corps Women's Reserve were also created for women performing auxiliary roles. The WAAC, however, never accomplished its goal of making available to "the national defense the knowledge, skill, and special training of the women of the nation." In July 1943, the WAAC was reorganized to form the Women's Army Corps, which was recognized as an official part of the regular army, but not in combat units. The Women's Army Corps replaced the Women's Army Auxiliary Corps. WAACs served overseas in North Africa in 1942. In 1944 WACs landed in Normandy after D-Day and served in Australia, New Guinea and the Philippines in the Pacific. During the war, 67 Army nurses and 11 Navy nurses were captured and spent three years as Japanese prisoners of war. 350,000 American women served during World War II and 16 were killed in action. Indeed, World War II also marked milestones for women in the US military, Carmen Contreras-Bozak, who became the first Hispanic to join the WAC, serving in Algiers under General Dwight D. Eisenhower and Minnie Spotted-Wolf the first Native American woman to enlist in the United States Marines. In 1943, the first female officer of the United States Marine Corps was commissioned, and the first detachment of female marines was sent to Hawaii for duty in 1945.

U.S. women also performed many kinds of non-military service in organizations such as the Women Airforce Service Pilots (WASP), Office of Strategic Services (OSS), American Red Cross, Cadet Nurse Corps, and the United Service Organizations (USO). Nineteen million American women filled out the home front labor force, not only as "Rosie the Riveters" in war factory jobs, but in transportation, agricultural, and office work of every variety. Women joined the federal government in massive numbers during World War II. Nearly a million "government girls" were recruited for war work. In addition, women volunteers aided the war effort by planting victory gardens, canning produce, selling war bonds, donating blood, salvaging needed commodities and sending care packages.

Treatment of women on the warfront

Although women became more involved in the military during World War II, they were not treated equally to men. Many commanding officers purposefully kept women out of combat. There were also cases in which men falsely accused women of promiscuity, although there were more cases where promiscuity was a factor.

After the war

The Second World War changed many things: it let women do the jobs that they wanted to do, and it let them compete in a man's world and made the men no longer 'masters of the house'. But at the end of World War II, most of the women lost their jobs because the men wanted them back. After the war, the women went back to doing the old jobs (housewives), and when needed, they helped the men in the harder jobs.

See also

- History of women in the military
- First Aid Nursing Yeomanry (UK) -known as "FANYs"
- Home front during World War II
- SPARS (USA)
- Women Accepted for Volunteer Emergency Service (USA) -known as "WAVES"
- Women Airforce Service Pilots (USA) -known as "WASPs"
- Women in the Russian and Soviet military
- Women's Army Corps (USA) -known as "WACs"
- Women's Auxiliary Air Force (UK)

- Women's Auxiliary Territorial Service (UK) (in which Princess Elizabeth, now Queen Elizabeth II was enlisted)
- Women's Royal Australian Naval Service (Australia) -known as "WRANS"
- Women's Royal Naval Service (UK) -known as "Wrens"
- Women's Royal Army Corps (UK)
- Air Transport Auxiliary (UK)
- Female guards in Nazi concentration camps
- Australian Women's Army Service (World War II)
- Australian Women's Land Army
- Woman's Land Army of America
- Women's Land Army (UK)
- Dorothy Lawrence British reporter who posed as a man in the First World War.

Bibliography

Women on the Homefront

- D'Ann Campbell, *Women at War With America: Private Lives in a Patriotic Era* (1984)
- Calder, Angus. *The People's War: Britain 1939-45* (1969)
- Costello, John. *Love, Sex, and War: Changing Values, 1939-1945* (1985). US title: *Virtue under Fire: How World War II Changed Our Social and Sexual Attitudes*
- Darian-Smith, Kate. *On the Home Front: Melbourne in Wartime, 1939-1945.* Australia: Oxford UP, 1990.
- Gildea, Robert. *Marianne in Chains: Daily Life in the Heart of France During the German Occupation* (2004)
- Maurine W. Greenwald. *Women, War, and Work: The Impact of World War I on Women Workers in the United States* (1990)
- Hagemann, Karen and Stefanie Schüler-Springorum; *Home/Front: The Military, War, and Gender in Twentieth-Century Germany.* Berg, 2002.
- Harris, Carol (2000). *Women at War 1939-1945: The Home Front*. Stroud: Sutton Publishing Limited. ISBN 0-7509-2536-1.
- Havens, Thomas R. "Women and War in Japan, 1937-1945." *American Historical Review* 80 (1975): 913-934. online in JSTOR.
- Higonnet, Margaret R., et al., eds. *Behind the Lines: Gender and the Two World Wars.* Yale UP, 1987.
- Marwick, Arthur. *War and Social Change in the Twentieth Century: A Comparative Study of Britain, France, Germany, Russia, and the United States.* 1974.
- Noakes, J. (ed.), *The Civilian in War: The Home Front in Europe, Japan and the U.S.A. in World War II.* Exeter: Exeter University Press. 1992.

- Pierson, Ruth Roach. *They're Still Women After All: The Second World War and Canadian Womanhood.* Toronto: McClelland and Stewart, 1986.
- Regis, Margaret. *When Our Mothers Went to War: An Illustrated History of Women in World War II.* [1] Seattle: NavPublishing. (2008) ISBN 978-1-87732-05-0.
- Wightman, Clare (1999). *More than Munitions: Women, Work and the Engineering Industries 1900-1950.* London: Addison Wesley Longman limited. ISBN 0-582-41435-0.
- Williams, Mari. A. (2002). *A Forgotten Army: Female Munitions Workers of South Wales, 1939-1945.* Cardiff: University of Wales Press. ISBN 0-7083-1726-X.

- "Government Girls of World War II" 2004 film by Leslie Sewell

Women in Military service

- Bidwell, Shelford. *The Women's Royal Army Corps* (London, 1977),
- Campbell, D'Ann. "Women in Combat: The World War Two Experience in the United States, Great Britain, Germany, and the Soviet Union" *Journal of Military History* (April 1993), 57:301-323. online edition [2]
- D'Ann Campbell, *Women at War With America: Private Lives in a Patriotic Era* (1984)
- D'Ann Campbell. "Women in Uniform: The World War II Experiment," *Military Affairs*, Vol. 51, No. 3, Fiftieth Year—1937-1987 (Jul., 1987), pp. 137–139 in JSTOR [3]
- Cottam, K. Jean, ed. *The Golden-Tressed Soldier* (Manhattan, KS, Military Affairs/Aerospace Historian Publishing, 1983) on Soviet women
- Cottam, K. Jean. *Soviet Airwomen in Combat in World War II* (Manhattan, KS: Military Affairs/Aerospace Historian Publishing, 1983)
- Cottam, K. Jean. "Soviet Women in Combat in World War II: The Ground Forces and the Navy," *International Journal of Women's Studies,* 3, no. 4 (1980): 345-57
- DeGroot G.J. "Whose Finger on the Trigger? Mixed Anti-Aircraft Batteries and the Female Combat Taboo," *War in History,* Volume 4, Number 4, December 1997, pp. 434–453(20)
- Dombrowski, Nicole Ann. *Women and War in the Twentieth Century: Enlisted With Or Without Consent* (1999)
- Regis, Margaret. *When Our Mothers Went to War: An Illustrated History of Women in World War II.* [1] Seattle: NavPublishing. (2008) ISBN 978-1-87732-05-0.
- Saywell, Shelley. *Women in War* (Toronto, 1985);
- Seidler, Franz W. *Frauen zu den Waffen—Marketenderinnen, Helferinnen Soldatinnen* ["Women to Arms: Sutlers, Volunteers, Female Soldiers"] (Koblenz, Bonn: Wehr & Wissen, 1978)
- Stoff, Laurie S. *They Fought for the Motherland: Russia's Women Soldiers in World War I And the Revolution* (2006)
- Treadwell, Mattie. *The Women's Army Corps* (1954)
- Tuten, "Jeff M. Germany and the World Wars," in Nancy Loring Goldman, ed. *Female Combatants or Non-Combatants?* (1982)

External links

- Women of World War I [4] The Women of World War I (from the book "War and Gender").
- Railwaywomen in Wartime [5] British women's work on the railways in both world wars - photos and text - free information.
- WWII US women's service organizations [6] — History and uniforms in color (WAAC/WAC, WAVES, ANC, NNC, USMCWR, PHS, SPARS, ARC and WASP)
- The U.S. Army Nurse Corps [7] a publication of the United States Army Center of Military History
- Women soldiers in Polish Home Army [8]
- Women in World War II Fact Sheet [9] Statistics on the many roles of American women in World War II

The Greatest Generation

Greatest Generation

"**The Greatest Generation**" is a term coined by journalist Tom Brokaw to describe the generation who grew up in the United States during the deprivation of the Great Depression, and then went on to fight in World War II, as well as those whose productivity within the war's home front made a decisive material contribution to the war effort. The generation is sometimes referred to as the *G.I. Generation* (a term coined by authors William Strauss and Neil Howe who are known for their generational theory). It follows the Lost Generation of the 1920s who fought in World War I and precedes the Silent Generation of the 1930s who grew up during World War II.

Tom Brokaw's book

Broadcast journalist Tom Brokaw wrote in his 1998 book *The Greatest Generation*, "it is, I believe, the greatest generation any society has ever produced."[1] He argued that these men and women fought not for fame and recognition, but because it was the right thing to do. When they came back they rebuilt America into a superpower. The book was a great popular success. Some critics and historians found the phenomenon overblown, or simplistic. Others felt an implied criticism of the Baby Boom Generation, and defended that generation's social values against those of the Greatest Generation.

In their 1991 book *Generations: The History of Americas Future, 1584 to 2069*, the historians William Strauss and Neil Howe define the "G.I. Generation" as the cohorts born in the United States from 1901 through 1924. This generation came of age during the Great Depression and World War II.

Famous members

- Creighton Abrams: (1914–1974), veteran of World War II, Korean War and general in the United States Army commanding military operations in the Vietnam War from 1968-72.
- Joe Foss: (1915–2003), WWII USMC fighter ace, Governor of South Dakota, featured prominently in Brokaw's book
- John F. Kennedy: (1917–1963), 35th President of the United States
- J. D. Salinger: (1919–2010), an author best known for the controversial 1951 novel, *The Catcher in the Rye*
- Robin Olds: (1922–2007), American fighter pilot, ace, general officer in the U.S. Air Force and veteran of World War II and Vietnam War.
- George H.W. Bush: (b.1924), 41st President of the United States

- Walter Cronkite: (1916–2009), reporter for CBS News from 1951 to 1997, one of eight journalists selected by the United States Army Air Forces to fly bombing raids over Germany in a B-17 Flying Fortress
- Joe DiMaggio: (1914–1999), famous player for the New York Yankees
- Eugene B. Fluckey: (1913–2007), United States Navy submarine commander who received the Medal of Honor during World War II
- Billy Graham: (b.1918), televangelist
- Ted Williams: (1915–2002), famous baseball player for Boston Red Sox, fought in WWII and Korean War
- Daniel Inouye: (b.1924), third longest-serving US Senator in history, officer in the 442nd Regimental Combat Team
- Richard Winters: (b.1918), WWII veteran of the 101st Airborne Division, famous for his portrayal in *Band of Brothers*
- Charles M. Schulz: (1922–2000), American cartoonist, served with U.S. 20th Armored Division in WWII
- Howard Keel: (1919–2004), American actor
- Ronald Reagan: (1911–2004), 40th President of the United States
- Jackie Robinson: (1919–1972), American Major League Baseball player, Civil Rights pioneer
- Benjamin O. Davis, Jr.: (1912–2002), United States Air Force General and commander of the World War II Tuskegee Airmen
- Eugene Sledge: (1923–2001), United States Marine who served in the Pacific Theater during WWII, specifically Peleliu and Okinawa. He documented his experience in his memoir, *With the Old Breed*. Certain material from the memoir was used by Ken Burns in his seven part documentary *The War*. It was also used by Tom Hanks and Steven Spielberg in their miniseries *The Pacific*.
- Lynn Compton: (b.1921), WWII Veteran of the 101st Airborne, famous for his portrayal in the *Band of Brothers* and for his prosecution of Sirhan Sirhan.
- Howard Zinn

See also
- Military history of the United States during World War II
- United States home front during World War II
- Great Depression in the United States
- List of generations

References

- *The Greatest Generation* by Tom Brokaw (1998) ISBN 0-375-50202-5 (hardback) ISBN 0-385-33462-1 (paperback), depicts the Americans who came of age during the Great Depression and fought World War II.
- *The Greatest Generation Speaks* by Tom Brokaw (1999) ISBN 0-375-50394-3 (hardback) ISBN 0-385-33538-5 (paperback)
- *The Great Boom 1950-2000: How a Generation of Americans Created the World's Most Prosperous Society* by Robert Sobel (2000) ISBN 0-312-20890-1
- *Generations: The History of America's Future, 1584 to 2069* by Strauss and Howe (1991) ISBN 0-688-11912-3

External links

- *Booknotes* interview with Tom Brokaw on *The Greatest Generation*, March 7, 1999. [2]
- *LifeCourse Associates* Generations in Anglo-American History [3]

The Home Front

United States home front during World War II

This page, **United States home front during World War II**, covers the developments within the United States, 1940–1945, to support its efforts during World War II.

Taxes and controls

Federal tax policy was highly contentious during the war, with Roosevelt battling a conservative Congress. Everyone agreed on the need for high taxes to pay for the war. Roosevelt tried unsuccessfully to increase tax on incomes over $25,000, while Congress enlarged the base downward. By 1944 nearly every employed person was paying federal income taxes (compared to 10% in 1940).

Many controls were put on the economy. The most important were price controls, imposed on most products and monitored by the Office of Price Administration. Wages were also controlled. In addition, the military imposed priorities that largely shaped industrial production.

Labor

The unemployment problem ended in the United States with the beginning of World War II, when stepped up wartime production created millions of new jobs and the draft pulled young men out.

Women also joined the workforce to replace men who had joined the forces, though in fewer numbers. Roosevelt stated that the efforts of civilians at home to support the war through personal sacrifice was as critical to winning the war as the efforts of the soldiers themselves. "Rosie the Riveter" became the symbol of women laboring in manufacturing. The war effort brought about significant changes in the role of women in society as a whole. At the end of the war, many of the munitions factories closed. Other women were replaced by returning veterans. However most women who wanted to continue working did so.

In the figure below the development of the United States labor force by gender during the war years.

Year	Total labor force (*1000)	of which Male (*1000)	of which Female (*1000)	Female share of total (%)
1940	56,100	41,940	14,160	25.2
1941	57,720	43,070	14,650	25.4
1942	60,330	44,200	16,120	26.7
1943	64,780	45,950	18,830	29.1
1944	66,320	46,930	19,390	29.2
1945	66,210	46,910	19,304	29.2
1946	60,520	43,690	16,840	27.8

Labor shortages were felt in agriculture, even though most farmers were given an occupational exemption and few were drafted. Large numbers volunteered or moved to cities for factory jobs. At the same time many agricultural commodities were more needed for the military and for the civilian populations of Allies. In some areas schools were temporarily closed at harvest time to enable students to work. Several hundred thousand enemy prisoners of war were used as farm laborers.

Labor unions

The war mobilization changed the relationship of the Congress of Industrial Organizations (CIO) with both employers and the national government; much less is known about the rival American Federation of Labor (AFL) during the war.

Welder making boilers for a ship, Combustion Engineering Co., Chattanooga, Tennessee. June 1942.

Nearly all the unions that belonged to the CIO were fully supportive of both the war effort and of the Roosevelt administration. However the Mine Workers, who had taken an isolationist stand in the years leading up to the war and had opposed Roosevelt's reelection in 1940, left the CIO in 1942. The CIO, in particular the United Auto Workers (UAW), supported a wartime no-strike pledge that aimed to eliminate not only major strikes for new contracts, but also the innumerable small strikes called by shop stewards and local union leadership to protest particular grievances.

The CIO did not, on the other hand, strike over wages during the war. In return for labor's no-strike pledge, the government offered arbitration to determine the wages and other terms of new contracts. Those procedures produced modest wage increases during the first few years of the war but not enough to keep up with inflation, particularly when combined with the slowness of the arbitration machinery.

Even though the complaints from union members about the no-strike pledge became louder and more bitter, the CIO did not abandon it. The Mine Workers, by contrast, who did not belong to either the AFL or the CIO for much of the war, engaged in a successful twelve-day strike in 1943.

But the CIO unions on the whole grew stronger during the war. The government put pressure on employers to recognize unions to avoid the sort of turbulent struggles over union recognition of the 1930s, while unions were generally able to obtain maintenance of membership clauses, a form of union security, through arbitration and negotiation. Workers also won benefits, such as vacation pay, that had been available only to a few in the past while wage gaps between higher skilled and less skilled workers narrowed.

The experience of bargaining on a national basis, while restraining local unions from striking, also tended to accelerate the trend toward bureaucracy within the larger CIO unions. Some, such as the Steelworkers, had always been centralized organizations in which authority for major decisions resided at the top. The UAW, by contrast, had always been a more grassroots organization, but it also started to try to rein in its maverick local leadership during these years.

The CIO also had to confront deep racial divides in its own membership, particularly in the UAW plants in Detroit where white workers sometimes struck to protest the promotion of black workers to production jobs, but also in shipyards in Alabama, mass transit in Philadelphia, and steel plants in Baltimore. The CIO leadership, particularly those in further left unions such as the Packinghouse Workers, the UAW, the NMU and the Transport Workers, undertook serious efforts to suppress hate strikes, to educate their membership and to support the Roosevelt Administration's tentative efforts to remedy racial discrimination in war industries through the Fair Employment Practices Commission. Those unions contrasted their relatively bold attack on the problem with the timidity and racism of the AFL.

The CIO unions were progressive in dealing with gender discrimination in wartime industry, which now employed many more women workers in nontraditional jobs. Unions that had represented large numbers of women workers before the war, such as the UE and the Food and Tobacco Workers, had fairly good records of fighting discrimination against women. Most union leaders saw women as temporary wartime replacements for the men in the armed forces. It was important that the wages of these women be kept high so that the veterans would get high wages.

Civilian support for war effort

The Civil Air Patrol was established, which enrolled civilian spotters in air reconnaissance, search-and-rescue, and transport. Its Coast Guard counterpart, the Coast Guard Auxiliary, used civilian boats and crews in similar roles. Towers were built in coastal and border towns, and spotters were trained to recognize enemy aircraft. Blackouts were practiced in every city, even those far from the coast. All lighting had to be extinguished to avoid helping the enemy in targeting at night. The main purpose was to remind people that there was a war on and to provide activities that would engage the civil spirit of millions of people not otherwise involved in the war effort. In large part, this effort was successful, sometimes almost to a fault, such as the Plains states where many dedicated aircraft spotters took up their posts night after night watching the skies in an area of the country that no enemy aircraft of that time could possibly hope to reach.

A synagogue on West Twenty-Third Street in New York City remained open 24 hours on D-Day for special services and prayer.

The United Service Organizations (USO) was founded in 1941 in response to a request from President Franklin D. Roosevelt to provide morale and recreation services to uniformed military personnel. This request led six civilian agencies—the Salvation Army, Young Men's Christian Association, Young Women's Christian Association, National Catholic Community Service, National Travelers Aid Association and the National Jewish Welfare Board—to unite in support of the troops. The United Service Organizations, or USO, was incorporated in New York on February 4, 1941.

Legions of women previously employed only in the home, or in traditionally female work, took jobs in factories that directly supported the war effort, or filled jobs vacated by men who had entered military service.

Draft

A female factory worker in 1942, Fort Worth, Texas. Women entered the workforce as men were drafted into the armed forces.

In 1940 Congress passed the first peace-time draft legislation, which was led by Grenville Clark. It was renewed (by one vote) in summer 1941. It involved questions as to who should control the draft, the size of the army, and the need for deferments. The system worked through local draft boards comprising community leaders who were given quotas and then decided how to fill them. There was very little draft resistance.

The nation went from a surplus manpower pool with high unemployment and relief in 1940 to a severe manpower shortage by 1943. Industry realized that the Army urgently desired production of essential war materials and foodstuffs more than soldiers. (Large numbers of soldiers were not used until the invasion of Europe in summer 1944.) In 1940-43 the Army often transferred soldiers to civilian status in the Enlisted Reserve Corps in order to increase production. Those transferred would return to work in essential industry, although they could be called back to active duty if the Army needed them. Others were discharged if their civilian work was deemed absolutely essential. There were instances of mass releases of men to increase production in various industries.

In the figure below an overview of the development of the United States labor force, the armed forces and unemployment during the war years.

Year	Total labor force (*1000)	Armed forces (*1000)	Unemployed (*1000)	Unemployment rate (%)
1939	55,588	370	9,480	17.2
1940	56,180	540	8,120	14.6
1941	57,530	1,620	5,560	9.9
1942	60,380	3,970	2,660	4.7
1943	64,560	9,020	1,070	1.9
1944	66,040	11,410	670	1.2
1945	65,290	11,430	1,040	1.9
1946	60,970	3,450	2,270	3.9

One contentious issue involved the drafting of fathers, which was avoided as much as possible. The drafting of 18-year olds was desired by the military but vetoed by public opinion. Supposedly, Blacks and Asians were drafted at the same rate as Whites.Wikipedia:Avoid weasel words The experience of

World War I regarding men needed by industry was particularly unsatisfactory—too many skilled mechanics and engineers became privates (there is a possibly apocryphal story of a *banker* assigned as a *baker* due to a clerical error, noted by historian Lee Kennett in his book "G.I."). Farmers demanded and were generally given occupational deferments (many volunteered anyway, but those who stayed at home lost postwar veteran's benefits.)

Later in the war, in light of the tremendous amount of manpower that would be necessary for the invasion of France, many earlier deferment categories became draft eligible.

Population movements

There was large-scale migration to industrial centers, especially on the West Coast. Millions of wives followed their husbands to military camps. Many new military training bases were established or enlarged, especially in the South. Large numbers of African Americans left the cotton fields and headed for the cities. Housing was increasingly difficult to find in industrial centers; commuting by car was limited by gasoline rationing. People car pooled or took public transportation, which was seriously overcrowded. Trains were heavily booked, so people limited vacation and long-distance travel.

Rationing

Main article: Rationing#United States

At the beginning of World War II, a rationing system was begun in the United States. Tires were the first item to be rationed in January 1942 because supplies of natural rubber were interrupted. Soon afterward, passenger automobiles, typewriters, sugar, gasoline, bicycles, footwear, fuel oil, coffee, stoves, shoes, meat, lard, shortening and oils, cheese, butter, margarine, processed foods (canned, bottled and frozen), dried fruits, canned milk, firewood and coal, jams, jellies and fruit butter, were rationed by November 1943.

To get a classification and a book of rationing stamps, one had to appear before a local rationing board. Each person in a household received a ration book, including babies and small children. When purchasing fuel, a driver had to present a gas card along with a ration book and cash. Ration stamps were valid only for a set period to forestall hoarding.

Role of women

Employment

Women took on an active role in World War II and took on many paid jobs in temporary new munitions factories and in old factories that had been converted from civilian products like automobiles. This was the "Rosie the Riveter" phenomenon.

They also filled many traditionally female jobs that were created by the war boom—as waitresses, for example. And they worked at jobs that previously had been held by men—such as bank teller or shoe salesperson. Nearly one million women worked as so called "government girls," taking jobs in the federal government, mainly in Washington, DC, that had previously been held by men or were newly created to deal with the war effort.

Riveting team working on the cockpit shell of a C-47 transport at the plant of North American Aviation. Office of War Information photo by Alfred T. Palmer, 1942.

During World War II, women began to gain more respect and men realized that women actually could work outside of the home. They fought for equal pay and made a huge impact on the United States workforce. They began to take over "male" jobs and gained confidence in themselves.

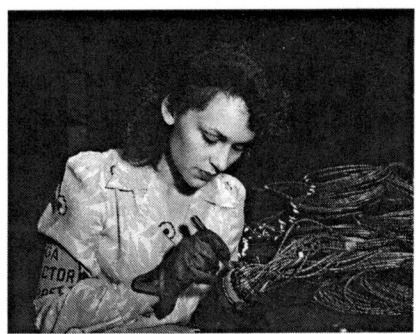

Woman aircraft worker checking assemblies. California, 1942.

In general when they replaced men they came with fewer skills. Industry retooled its machine jobs so that unskilled workers could handle them. (This opened many jobs for men who had been unemployed in the 1930s.) Some unions tried to maintain the same pay scale as men had because they expected men to resume their jobs after the war. At the Oak Ridge plant separating

U-235 for the Manhattan Project, it was noted that the girl "hill-billy" operators employed by Tennessee Eastman outperformed the scientists first used on the calutrons.

Volunteer activities

Women staffed millions of jobs in community service roles, such as nursing, USO, and Red Cross while the men were at war.

Women Airforce Service Pilots

The Women Airforce Service Pilots, also known as WASP, and the predecessor groups the Women's Flying Training Detachment (WFTD) and the Women's Auxiliary Ferrying Squadron (WAFS) (official from September 10, 1942) were each a pioneering organization of civilian female pilots employed to fly military aircraft under the direction of the United States Army Air Forces during gender-sensitive days of World War II that eventually would number in the thousands of female pilots, each freeing up a male pilot for combat service and duties. The WFTD and WAFS were combined on August 5, 1943 to create the para-military WASP organization.

Woman standing next to a wide range of tire sizes required by military aircraft.

Baby boom

Marriage and motherhood came back as prosperity empowered couples who had postponed marriage. The birth rate started shooting up in 1941, paused in 1944-45 as 12 million men were in uniform, then continued to soar until reaching a peak in the late 1950s. This was the "Baby Boom."

In a New Deal-like move, the federal government set up the "EMIC" program that provided free prenatal and natal care for the wives of servicemen below the rank of sergeant.

Housing shortages, especially in the munitions centers, forced millions of couples to live with parents or in makeshift facilities. Little housing had been built in the Depression years, so the shortages grew steadily worse until about 1948, when a massive housing boom finally caught up with demand. (After 1944 much of the new housing was supported by the G.I. Bill.)

Federal law made it difficult to divorce absent servicemen, so the number of divorces peaked when they returned in 1946. In long-range terms, divorce rates changed little.

Housewives

Juggling their roles as mothers due to the Baby Boom and the jobs they filled while the men were at war, women strained to complete all tasks set before them. The war caused cutbacks in automobile and bus service, and migration from farms and towns to munitions centers. Those housewives who worked found the dual role difficult to handle.

The worst psychological pressure came when sons, husbands, fathers, brothers and fiances were drafted and sent to faraway training camps, preparing for a war in which nobody knew how many would be killed. Millions of wives tried to relocate near their husbands' training camps.

Role of minorities

FEPC

The FEPC was a federal executive order requiring companies with government contracts not to discriminate on the basis of race or religion. It assisted African Americans in obtaining jobs in industry. Under pressure from A. Philip Randolph's growing March on Washington Movement, on June 25, 1941, President Roosevelt created the Fair Employment Practices Committee (FEPC) by signing Executive Order 8802. It said "there shall be no discrimination in the employment of workers in defense industries or government because of race, creed, color, or national origin". In 1943 Roosevelt greatly strengthened FEPC with a new executive order, #9346. It required that all government contracts have a non-discrimination clause. FEPC was the most significant breakthrough ever for Blacks and women on the job front. During the war the federal government operated airfield, shipyards, supply centers, ammunition plants and other facilities that employed millions. FEPC rules applied and guaranteed equality of employment rights. Of course, these facilities shut down when the war ended. In the private sector the FEPC was generally successful in enforcing non-discrimination in the North, it did not attempt to challenge segregation in the South, and in the border region its intervention led to hate strikes by angry white workers.

African American: Double V campaign

The African American community in the United States resolved on a Double V Campaign: Victory over fascism abroad, and victory over discrimination at home. Large numbers migrated from poor Southern farms to munitions centers. Racial tensions were high in overcrowded cities like Chicago; Detroit and Harlem experienced race riots in 1943.The derogative name jig was coined during this time. The *Pittsburgh Courier* created the Double V Campaign after readers began commenting on their second class status during wartime.

Internment of Japanese Americans

Main article: Japanese American internment

In 1942 the War Department demanded that all enemy nationals be removed from war zones on the West Coast. The question became how to evacuate the estimated 120,000 people of Japanese citizenship living in California. Roosevelt looked at the secret evidence available to him: the Japanese in the Philippines had collaborated with the Japanese invasion troops; most of the adult Japanese in California had been strong supporters of Japan in the war against China. There was evidence of espionage compiled by code-breakers that decrypted messages to Japan from agents in North America and Hawaii before and after the attack on Pearl Harbor. These MAGIC cables were kept secret from all but those with the highest clearance, such as Roosevelt. On February 19, 1942, Roosevelt signed Executive Order 9066 which set up designated military areas "from which any or all persons may be excluded." The most controversial part of the order included American born children and youth who had dual U.S. and Japanese citizenship.

In addition to the Japanese, thousands of civilian Germans and Italians were interned; some with their families, some taken from their families. They were given hearing, but had no representation of their own. These internees were picked up by the FBI based on records compiled prior to and at the beginning of the War.

In February 1943, when activating the 442nd Regimental Combat Team—a unit composed mostly of American-born American citizens of Japanese descent living in Hawaii—Roosevelt said, "No loyal citizen of the United States should be denied the democratic right to exercise the responsibilities of his citizenship, regardless of his ancestry. The principle on which this country was founded and by which it has always been governed is that Americanism is a matter of the mind and heart; Americanism is not, and never was, a matter of race or ancestry." In 1944, the U.S. Supreme Court upheld the legality of the executive order in the *Korematsu v. United States* case. The executive order remained in force until December when Roosevelt released the Japanese internees, except for those who announced their intention to return to Japan.

Italy was an official enemy, and citizens of Italy were also forced away from "strategic" coastal areas in California. Altogether, 58,000 Italians were forced to relocate. They relocated on their own and were not put in camps. Known spokesmen for Mussolini were arrested and held in prison. The restrictions were dropped in October 1942, and Italy switched sides in 1943 and became an American ally. In the east, however, the large Italian populations of the northeast, especially in munitions-producing centers such as Bridgeport and New Haven faced no restrictions and contributed just as much to the war effort as other Americans.

Wartime politics

Roosevelt easily won the bitterly contested 1940 election, but the Conservative coalition maintained a tight grip on Congress. Wendell Willkie, the defeated GOP candidate in 1940, became a roving ambassador for Roosevelt. After a series of squabbles with Vice President Henry A. Wallace, Roosevelt stripped him of his administrative responsibilities and dropped him from the 1944 ticket, choosing instead Senator Harry S. Truman. Truman was best known for investigating waste, fraud and inefficiency in civilian programs. In very light turnout in 1942 the Republicans made major gains. In the 1944 election, Roosevelt defeated Tom Dewey in a relatively close race that attracted little attention.

Propaganda and culture

The media cooperated with the federal government in presenting the official view of the war. All movie scripts had to be pre-approved. World War II posters helped to mobilize the nation. Inexpensive, accessible, and ever-present, the poster was an ideal agent for making war aims the personal mission of every citizen. Government agencies, businesses, and private organizations issued an array of poster images linking the military front with the home front—calling upon every American to boost production at work and at home. Deriving their appearance from the fine and commercial

Rural school children in front of homefront posters. San Augustine County, Texas. 1943.

arts, posters conveyed more than simple slogans. Posters expressed the needs and goals of the people who created them. By definition, wartime posters are naturally propagandistic, but most posters were merely patriotically so. Some, however, resorted to extreme racial and ethnic caricatures of the enemy, sometimes as hopelessly bumbling cartoon characters, sometimes as evil, half-human creatures. The National Archives, Northwestern University and the University of Minnesota all have extensive collections of World War II posters accessible online that contain many examples of posters of the era in regard to the use of propaganda, both subtle and patriotic, and blatantly anti-German and Japanese.

One of the most noteworthy areas of civilian involvement during the war was in the area of recycling. Many everyday commodities were vital to the war effort, and drives were organized to recycle such things as rubber, tin, waste kitchen fats (the predominant raw material of explosives and many pharmaceuticals) paper, lumber, steel and many others. Popular phrases promoted by the government at the time were "Get into the scrap!" and "Get some cash for your trash" (a nominal sum was paid to the donor for many kinds of scrap items) and Thomas "Fats" Waller even wrote and recorded a song with the latter title. Such commodities as rubber and tin remained highly important as recycled materials until the end of the war, while others, such as steel, were critically needed at first, but in lesser quantities as damaged war supplies were returned from overseas for scrapping, lessening the need for civilian scrap metal drives. Once again, war propaganda played a prominent role in many of these drives.

A strong aspect of American culture then as now was a fascination with celebrities, and many stars of Hollywood and radio gave service above and beyond the call in the donation of their time for everything from being Civilian Defense marshals to making personal appearances at War Bond drives. Bonds were the money that financed the war, and Bond drives where celebrities appeared were always very successful. Several stars were responsible for personal appearance tours that netted multiple millions of dollars in bond pledges—an astonishing amount in 1943. The public paid 3/4 of the face value of a war bond, and received the full face value back after a set number of years. While this may have represented a rather unspectacular interest rate, the government has never defaulted on payment of any mature bond. People were challenged to put "at least 10% of every paycheck into Bonds". Compliance was very high, with entire factories of workers earning a special "Minuteman" flag to fly over their plant if all workers belonged to the "Ten Percent Club". There were seven major War Loan drives, all of which exceeded their goals. An added advantage was that citizens who were putting their money into War Bonds were not putting it into the home front wartime economy. There was a job for anyone who wanted one during the war, most of them well-paid. Personal income was at an all-time high, and more dollars were chasing fewer goods to purchase. This was a recipe for economic disaster that was largely avoided because Americans—cajoled daily by their government to do so—were also saving money at an all-time high rate, mostly in War Bonds but also in private savings accounts and insurance policies.

Hollywood studios also went all-out for the war effort, as studios allowed their major stars (such as Clark Gable and James Stewart) to enlist, and also created propaganda films to remind American moviegoers of their heritage. Many of the finest films of the era are about the war, such as *Casablanca*, *Mrs. Miniver*, and *Going My Way*, while others, such as *Yankee Doodle Dandy*, focused on patriotism. Even before active American involvement in the war, the popular Three Stooges comic trio were lampooning the Nazi German leadership, and Nazis in general, with a number of short subject films, starting with *You Nazty Spy!* in January 1940, nearly two years before the United States was drawn into World War II, the very first Hollywood-produced work to ridicule Hitler and the Nazis.

Cartoons and short subjects were a major sign of the times, as Warner Brothers Studios and Disney Studios gave unprecedented aid to the war effort by creating cartoons that were both wildly patriotic (and very funny), and also contributed to remind movie-goers of important wartime activities such as rationing and scrap drives, war bond purchases, and the creation of victory gardens. Warner shorts such as Draftee Daffy, Russian Rhapsody and Daffy - The Commando are particularly remembered for their biting wit and unflinching mockery of the enemy (particularly Adolf Hitler, Hideki Tōjō and Hermann Goering. Their cartoons of Private Snafu, produced for the military as "training films", served to remind many military men of the importance of following proper procedure during wartime, for their own safety. Hanna Barbara also contributed to the war effort with slyly pro US short cartoon The Yankee Doodle Mouse with "Lt" Jerry Mouse as the hero and Tom Cat as the "enemy".

Walt Disney's studio also helped the war effort, as almost every cartoon produced by Disney in this period dealt with the war effort. Each Disney cartoon began with a headshot of Mickey Mouse, Donald Duck, or Goofy, and during this time each wore an Army or Navy cap. Disney produced a B-Feature based on the book, Victory Through Air Power and several promotional and comical shorts on the importance of rationing, buying bonds and paying one's income tax ("Taxes Against the Axis"). Education for Death was a Disney short documentary based on the book of the same name, on the making of a Nazi; demonstrating the cruelty of Hitler's Reich against even its own citizens, weeding out the "weak or inferior" and breeding hatred and obedience in its people, devoid of compassion. *Der Fuehrer's Face* aka *Donald Duck in Nutziland*, starring Donald living a nightmare in German province and working in a munitions plant, was one of the most popular and famous cartoons of the period. The song from the cartoon - "Der Fuehrer's face" recorded by Spike Jones & the City Slickers - also became very popular for its contempt of Nazi leaders:

> *Ven der Fuehrer says, "Ve iss der master race,"*
>
> *Ve HEIL! [honk!] HEIL! [honk!] Right in der Fuehrer's face!*
>
> *Not to luff der Fuehrer iss a great disgrace,*
>
> *So Ve HEIL! [honk!] HEIL! [honk!] Right in der Fuehrer's face!*
>
> *Ven Herr Goebbels says, "Ve own der world und space,"*
>
> *Ve HEIL! [honk!] HEIL! [honk!] Right in Herr Goebbels' face!*
>
> *Ven Herr Goering says, "Dey'll never bomb dis place,"*
>
> *Ve HEIL! [honk!] HEIL! [honk!] Right in Herr Goering's face!*

Disney's famous Three Little Pigs song "Who's Afraid of the Big, Bad Wolf" became a rallying cry for civilians during the war. In a short during the war years, the familiar pigs and wolf were re-imagined with the "bricks" in the Practical Pig's house being actually made of war bonds, and the Big Bad Wolf is shown wearing a swastika, representing Nazi Germany.

Disney Cartoon Mascots during the War:

- Donald Duck-mascot of United States Coast Guard Auxiliary; 309th Fighter Squadron; 415th Fighter Squadron; 438th Fighter Squadron; 479th Bombardment Squadron; 531st Bombardment Squadron.
- Goofy-mascot of 602nd Bomb Squadron; 756th Bomb Squadron.
- Pete (Disney character)-mascot of United States Merchant Marine; 603rd Bomb Squadron
- Figaro (Disney) mascot of RAF Ace Ian Gleed's Spitfire Mk. Vb Trop while he was in action over the Western Desert and the Mediterranean during the middle of the war.

The American Volunteer Group's "Flying Tiger" insignia, shown on a Curtiss P-40 fighter of that unit, piloted by ace Robert "R.T." Smith, was created by the Walt Disney Company.

The Disney company also created a number of military unit insignias for the United States forces during World War II, with one of hte best known ones being that of the American Volunteer Group, the well-known "Flying Tigers" of the China-Burma-India Theater's early years in the war.

The equally popular Looney Tunes characters of the time, from the Warner Brothers animation studio, also were used by a number of American military units, and individual fighting vehicles (mostly tanks, jeeps and warplanes), such as:

- Bugs Bunny-mascot of Kingman Army Air Field, Kingman, Arizona; 486th Bomb squadron; 530th Bombardment Squadron
- Daffy Duck-mascot of 600th Bomb Squadron
- Sylvester (Looney Tunes)-mascot of 45th Reconnaissance Squadron
- Yosemite Sam-mascot of US Army air Corps 20th Reconnaissance Squadron {later the 20th Intelligence Squadron}

See also

- American Minority Groups in World War II
- American music during World War II
- Greatest Generation
- Home front during World War II
- Military history of the United States during World War II
- Rosie the Riveter
- Rosie the Riveter/World War II Home Front National Historical Park
- Women Airforce Service Pilots
- Woman's Land Army of America
- Propaganda films:

- *Black Marketing*
- *Campus on the March*
- *Henry Browne, Farmer*
- *Manpower*
- *Negro Colleges in War Time*
- *The Arm Behind the Army*
- United States home front during World War I

References

- Brinkley, David. *Washington Goes to War* Knopf, 1988.
- Campbell, D'Ann (1984), *Women at War with America: Private Lives in a Patriotic Era* Harvard University Press.
- Cantril, Hadley and Mildred Strunk, eds.; *Public Opinion, 1935-1946* (1951), massive compilation of many public opinion polls from USA
- Ferguson, Robert G. "One Thousand Planes a Day: Ford, Grumman, General Motors and the Arsenal of Democracy." *History and Technology* 2005 21(2): 149-175. ISSN 0734-1512 Fulltext in Swetswise, Ingenta and Ebsco
- Flynn, George Q. *The Draft, 1940-1973* (1993) (ISBN 0-7006-1105-3)
- Gallup, George Horace, ed. *The Gallup Poll; Public Opinion, 1935-1971* 3 vol (1972) esp vol 1. summarizes results of each poll as reported to newspapers
- Garfinkel, Herbert . *When Negroes March: The March on Washington and the Organizational Politics for FEPC* (1959).
- Koistinen, Paul A. C. *Arsenal of World War II: The Political Economy of American Warfare, 1940–1945* (2004)
- Miller, Sally M., and Daniel A. Cornford eds. *American Labor in the Era of World War II* (1995), essays by historians, mostly on California
- Lichtenstein, Nelson. *Labor's War at Home: The CIO in World War II* (2003)
- Wynn, Neil A. *The Afro-American and the Second World War* (1977)
- Vatter, Howard. *The U.S. Economy in World War II* Columbia University Press, 1985. General survey

Further reading

Surveys

- Michael C.C. Adams. *The Best War Ever: America and World War II* (1993); contains detailed bibliography
- Blum, John Morton *V Was for Victory: Politics and American Culture During World War II* (1995; original edition (1976)
- Kennedy, David M. *Freedom from Fear: The American People in Depression and War, 1929-1945.*
- Polenberg, Richard. *War and Society: The United States, 1941-1945* (1980)
- Resch, John Phillips et al. eds. *Americans at War: Society, Culture, and the Homefront* vol 3 (2005), an encyclopedia
- Winkler, Allan M. *Home Front U.S.A.: America During World War II* (1986). short survey
- *10 Eventful Years: 1937-1946* 4 vol. Encyclopædia Britannica, 1947. Highly detailed encyclopedia of events

Economy and labor

- Aruga, Natsuki. "'An' Finish School': Child Labor during World War II." *Labor History* 29 (1988): 498-530. in JSTOR
- Campbell, D'Ann. "Sisterhood versus the Brotherhoods: Women in Unions"
- Dubofsky, Melvyn and Warren Van Time *John L. Lewis* (1986). Biography of head of coal miners' union
- Evans Paul. "The Effects of General Price Controls in the United States during World War II." *Journal of Political Economy* 90 (1983): 944-66. statistical in JSTOR
- Faue, Elizabeth. *Community of Suffering & Struggle: Women, Men, and the Labor Movement in Minneapolis, 1915-1945* (1991), social history
- Feagin, Joe R., and Kelly Riddell. "The State, Capitalism and World War II: The U.S. Case." *Armed Forces and Society* 17 (fall 1990): 53-79. in JSTOR
- George Q. Flynn; *The Mess in Washington: Manpower Mobilization in World War II* Greenwood Press. 1979.
- Fraser, Steve. *Labor Will Rule: Sidney Hillman and the Rise of American Labor* (1993). leader of CIO
- Harrison, Mark. "Resource Mobilization for World War II: The U.S.A., UK, U.S.S.R. and Germany, 1938-1945." *Economic History Review* 41 (1988): 171-92. in JSTOR
- Maines, Rachel. "Wartime Allocation of Textiles and Apparel Resources: Emergency Policy in the Twentieth Century." *Public Historian* 7 (1985): 29-51.
- Mills, Geofrey, and Hugh Rockoff. "Compliance with Price Controls in the United States and the United Kingdom during World War II." *Journal of Economic History* 47 (1987): 197-213. in JSTOR

- Reagan, Patrick D. "The Withholding Tax, Beardsley Ruml, and Modern American Public Policy." *Prologue* 24 (1992): 19-31.
- Rockoff, Hugh. "The Response of the Giant Corporations to Wage and Price Controls in World War II." *Journal of Economic History* 41 (1981): 123-28. in JSTOR
- Romer, Christina D. "What Ended the Great Depression?" *Journal of Economic History* 52 (1992): 757-84. in JSTOR
- Tuttle, William M., Jr. "The Birth of an Industry: The Synthetic Rubber 'Mess' in World War II." *Technology and Culture* 22 (1981): 35-67. in JSTOR
- Wilcox, Walter W. *The Farmer in the Second World War.* 1947 online [1].

Draft

- Bennett, Scott H., ed., Army GI, Pacifist CO: The World War II Letters of Frank and Albert Dietrich (New York: Fordham Univ. Press, 2005).
- Blum, Albert A. *Drafted Or Deferred: Practices Past and Present* Ann Arbor: Bureau of Industrial Relations, Graduate School of Business Administration, University of Michigan, 1967.
- Flynn George Q. "American Medicine and Selective Service in World War II." *Journal of the History of the Behavioral Sciences* 42 (1987): 305-26.

Gender and minorities

- Beth Bailey and David Farber; "The 'Double-V' Campaign in World War II Hawaii: African Americans, Racial Ideology, and Federal Power, " *Journal of Social History* Volume: 26. Issue: 4. 1993. pp 817+.
- Daniel, Clete. *Chicano Workers and the Politics of Fairness: The FEPC in the Southwest, 1941-1945* University of Texas Press, 1991
- William J. Collins, "Race, Roosevelt, and Wartime Production: Fair Employment in World War II Labor Markets," *American Economic Review* 91:1 (March 2001), pp. 272–286. in JSTOR
- John Costello. *Virtue Under Fire: How World War II Changed Our Social and Sexual Attitudes* (1986), US and Britain
- Susan M. Hartmann. *Home Front and Beyond: American Women in the 40's* (1982)
- Daniel Kryder.*Divided Arsenal: Race and the American State During World War II* (2001)
- Lees, Lorraine M. "National Security and Ethnicity: Contrasting Views during World War II." *Diplomatic History* 11 (1987): 113-25.
- Gunnar Myrdal, *An American Dilemma: The Negro Problem and Modern Democracy* (1944)
- *Records of the Women's Bureau* (1997), short essay on women at work [2]
- Barbara McLean Ward, ed., *Produce and Conserve, Share and Play Square: The Grocer and the Consumer on the Home-Front Battlefield during World War II*, Portsmouth, NH: Strawbery Banke Museum

- Ann Elizabeth Pfau, *Miss Yourlovin: GIs, Gender, and Domesticity during World War II* (New York: Columbia University Press, 2008) [3]

Politics

- Burns, James MacGregor. *Roosevelt: Soldier of Freedom* (1970), vol 2 covers the war years.
- Goodwin, Doris Kearns. *No Ordinary Time: Franklin and Eleanor Roosevelt: The Home Front in World War II* (1995)
- Graham, Otis L. and Meghan Robinson Wander, eds. *Franklin D. Roosevelt: His Life and Times.* (1985). encyclopedia
- Hooks Gregory. *The Military Industrial Complex: World War II's Battle of the Potomac* University of Illinois Press, 1991.
- Jeffries John W. "The 'New' New Deal: FDR and American Liberalism, 1937-1945." *Political Science Quarterly* (1990): 397-418. in JSTOR
- Leff Mark H. "The Politics of Sacrifice on the American Home Front in World War II." *Journal of American History* 77 (1991): 1296-1318.
- Rhodes Richard. *The Making of the Atomic Bomb* Simon & Schuster, 1986.
- Steele Richard W. "The Great Debate: Roosevelt, the Media, and the Coming of the War, 1940-1941." *Journal of American History* 71 (1994): 69-92.

Propaganda, advertising, media, public opinion

- Bredhoff, Stacey (1994), *Powers of Persuasion: Poster Art from World War II,* National Archives Trust Fund Board.
- Fox, Frank W (1975), *Madison Avenue Goes to War: The Strange Military Career of American Advertising, 1941–45,* Brigham Young University Press.
- Fyne, robert (1994), *The Hollywood Propaganda of World War II,* Scarecrow Press.
- Gregory, G.H. (1993), *Posters of World War II,* Gramercy Books.
- Gallup, George H. (1972), *The Gallup Poll: Public Opinion 1935- 1971, Vol. 1, 1935–1948,* short summary of every poll
- M. Paul Holsinger and Mary Anne Schofield; *Visions of War: World War II in Popular Literature and Culture* (1992) online edition [4]
- Terrence H. Witkowski; "World War II Poster Campaigns: Preaching Frugality to American Consumers" *Journal of Advertising*, Vol. 32, 2003

Social, state and local history

- Brown DeSoto. *Hawaii Goes to War. Life in Hawaii from Pearl Harbor to Peace.* 1989.
- Clive Alan. *State of War: Michigan in World War II* University of Michigan Press, 1979.
- Daniel Pete. "Going among Strangers: Southern Reactions to World War II." *Journal of American History* 77 (1990): 886-911.
- Gleason Philip. "Pluralism, Democracy, and Catholicism in the Era of World War II." *Review of Politics* 49 (1987): 208-30.
- Hartzel, Karl Drew. *The Empire State At War* (1949), on upstate New York online edition [5]
- Johnson Marliynn S. "War as Watershed: The East Bay and World War II." *Pacific Historical Review* 63 (1994): 315-41.
- T. A Larson. *Wyoming's war years, 1941-1945* (1993)
- Lichtenstein Nelson. "The Making of the Postwar Working Class: Cultural Pluralism and Social Structure in World War II." *Historian* 51 (1988): 42-63.
- Lee James Ward, Carolyn N. Barnes, and Kent A. Bowman, eds. *1941: Texas Goes to War* University of North Texas Press, 1991.
- Miller Marc. *The Irony of Victory. World War II and Lowell, Massachusetts* University of Illinois Press, 1988.
- Nash Gerald D. *The American West Transformed. The Impact of the Second World War* Indiana University Press, 1985.
- Smith C. Calvin. *War and Wartime Changes: The Transformation of Arkansas, 1940–1945* University of Arkansas Press, 1986.
- Tuttle Jr. William M.; *Daddy's Gone to War: The Second World War in the Lives of America's Children* Oxford University Press, 1995 online edition [6]
- O'Brien, Kenneth Paul and Lynn Hudson Parsons, eds. *The Home-Front War: World War II and American Society* (1995) online [7] essays by scholars
- Watters, Mary. *Illinois in the Second World War.* 2 vol (1951)

External links

- Regional Oral History Office / Rosie the Riveter / WWII American Homefront Project [8]
- American Anti-Axis Propaganda from WWII [9]
- Academic Data Related to the Roosevelt Administration [10]
- FDR Cartoon Archive [11]
- National Museum of the Civil Air Patrol (online, WWII section) [12]
- Powers of Persuasion: Poster Art from World War II, National Archives [13]
- Northwestern U Library World War II Poster Collection [14]
- War Ration Book Records and Related Information [15]
- (1999) Oxford History of the U.S. [16]

- 1942 The Navy Wife Wedding Etiquette [17]
- 1943 Arms and The Girl Wedding Etiquette [18]

Women in The Workforce

Women in the workforce

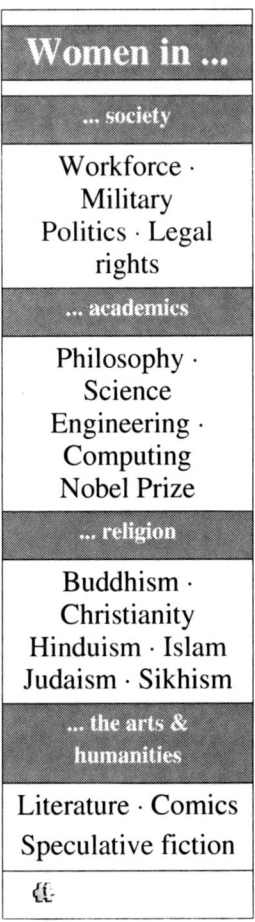

Women in ...
... society
Workforce · Military Politics · Legal rights
... academics
Philosophy · Science Engineering · Computing Nobel Prize
... religion
Buddhism · Christianity Hinduism · Islam Judaism · Sikhism
... the arts & humanities
Literature · Comics Speculative fiction

Until modern industrialized times, legal and cultural practices, combined with the inertia of longstanding religious and educational traditions, had restricted **women's entry and participation in the workforce**. Economic dependency upon men, and consequently the poor socio-economic status of women had also restricted their entry into the workforce. Particularly as occupations have become professionalized over the 19th and 20th centuries, women's access to higher education had effectively excluded them from the practice of well-paid and high status occupations. Entry of women into the higher professions like law and medicine was delayed in most countries due to women being denied entry to universities and qualification for degrees. For example, Cambridge University only fully validated degrees for women late in 1947, and even then only after much opposition and acrimonious debate. Such factors had largely limited women to low-paid and poor status occupations for most of the 19th and 20th centuries. However, through the 20th century, public perceptions of paid work shifted as the workforce increasingly moved to office jobs that do not require heavy labor, and women increasingly acquired the higher education that led to better-compensated, longer-term careers rather than lower-skilled, shorter-term jobs.

Restrictions on women's access to and participation in the workforce include the wage gap and the glass ceiling, inequities most identified with industrialized nations with nominal equal opportunity laws; legal and cultural restrictions on access to education and jobs, inequities most identified with developing nations; and unequal access to capital, variable but identified as a difficulty in both industrialized and developing nations.

Although access to paying occupations (the "workforce") has been and remains unequal in many occupations and places around the world, scholars sometimes distinguish "work" from "paying work." Analyses distinguishing between unpaid work and paying work have led to the frequently cited slogan "Women do two-thirds of the world's work, receive 10 percent of the world's income, and own 1 percent of the means of production", which has come to capture the imbalance between work and remuneration faced by women. This analysis considers uncompensated household labor — for instance, childcare, eldercare, and family subsistence farming — as well as compensated work in the workforce.

Areas of study

The division of labor by gender has been particularly studied in women's studies (especially women's history, which has frequently examined the history and biography of women's participation in particular fields) and gender studies more broadly. Occupational studies, such as the history of medicine or studies of professionalization, also examine questions of gender, and the roles of women in the history of particular fields.

In addition, modern civil rights law has frequently examined gender restrictions of access to a field of occupation; gender discrimination within a field; and gender harassment in particular workplaces. This body of law is called employment discrimination law, and gender and race discrimination are the largest sub-sections within the area. Laws specifically aimed at preventing discrimination against women have been passed in many countries; see, e.g., the Pregnancy Discrimination Act in the United States.

History and present-day status of women in the workforce

The 1870 US Census was the first US Census to count "Females engaged in each occupation" and provides an intriguing snapshot of women's history. It reveals that, contrary to popular belief, not all American women of the Victorian period were either idle in their middle class homes or working in sweatshops. Women were 15% of the total work force (1.8 million out of 12.5). They made up one-third of factory "operatives," but teaching and the occupations of dressmaking, millinery, and tailoring played a larger role. Two-thirds of teachers were women. Women could also be found in such unexpected places as iron and steel works (495), mines (46), sawmills (35), oil wells and refineries (40), gas works (4), and charcoal kilns (5) and held such surprising jobs as ship rigger (16), teamster (196), turpentine laborer (185), brass founder/worker (102), shingle and lathe maker (84), stock-herder (45), gun and locksmith (33), hunter and trapper (2).

In the beginning of the 20th century women were regarded as the guardians of morality; they were seen as made finer than men and were expected to act as such their role was not defined as workers or money makers. Women were expected to hold on to their innocence until the right man came along so that they can start a family and inculcate that morality they were in charge of preserving. Yet at the turn of the 20th century, a civil war changed America was now educating their women more and more. By 1900, four out of five colleges accepted women and a whole coed concept was becoming more and more accepted. In the United States, it was World War I that made space for women in the workforce amongst other economical and social influences. Due to the rise in demand for production from Europe during the raging war, women found themselves working outside the home. In the first quarter of the century, women mostly occupied jobs in factory work or as domestic servants, as the war come to an end they were able to move on to such jobs as: salespeople in department stores as well as clerical, secretarial and other, what is called, "lace-collar" jobs. . In July 1920, The New York Times ran a head line that read: "the American Woman ... has lifted her skirts far beyond any modest limitation" which could apply to more than just fashion; women were now rolling up their sleeves and skirts and making their way into the workforce.

World War II allowed for millions of jobs for women. Thousands of women actually joined the military: 140,000 in the Women's Army Corps (United States Army) WAC; 100,000 in the Navy (WAVE); 23,000 in the Marines; 14,000 in the Navy Nurse Corps and, 13,000 in the Coast Guard. Although almost none saw combat, they replaced men in non combative positions and got the same pay as the men would have on the same job. At the same time over 16 million men left their jobs to join the war in Europe and elsewhere, opening even more opportunities and places for women to take over in the job force.

The Quiet Revolution

The increase of women in the labor force gained momentum in the late 19th century. At this point women married early on and were defined by their marriages. If they entered the workforce it was only out of necessity. This in turn explained why most women in the labor force were lower class.

The gradual change that took off after this point can be broken down into four phases, the first three being evolutionary phases, moving slowly and spanning many years. The last phase is revolutionary because it took off quickly and in a short period of time. The last phase is most commonly known as **The Quiet Revolution**.

The first phase encompasses the time between the late 19th century to the 1920s. This era gave birth to the 'Independent female worker.' Before this time women in the workforce were typically young and unmarried. They had little or no learning on the job and typically held clerical and teaching positions. Women promptly exited the work force when they were married. Towards the end of the 1920s, as we enter into the second phase, married women begin to exit the work force less and less. Labor force productivity for married women 35–44 years of age increase by 15.5 percentage points from 10% to 25%. There was a greater demand for clerical positions and as the number of women graduating high school increased they began to hold more 'respectable', steady jobs. This phase has been appropriately labeled as the Transition Era referring to the time period between 1930-1950. During this time the discriminatory institution of marriage bars, which forced women out of the work force after marriage, were eliminated, allowing more participation in the work force of single and married women. However, still women's work was contingent upon their husband's income. Women did not normally work to fulfill a personal need to define ones career and social worth; they worked out of necessity.

In the third phase, labeled the "roots of the revolution" encompassing the time from 1950- mid-to-late 1970s, the movement began to approach the warning signs of a revolution. Women's expectations of future employment changed. Women began to see themselves going on to college and working through their marriages and even attending graduate school. Many however still had brief and intermittent work force participation, without necessarily having expectations for a 'career'. Although more women attended college, it was often expected that they attended to find a spouse—the so-called "M.R.S. degree". Nevertheless, Labor force participation by women still grew significantly.

The fourth phase, known as The Quiet Revolution, began in the late 1970s and continues on today. Beginning in the 1970s women began to flood colleges and grad schools. They began to enter profession like medicine, law, dental and business. More women were going to college and expected to be employed at the age of 35, as opposed to past generations that only worked intermittently due to marriage and childbirth. This increase in expectations of long-term gainful employment is reflected in the change of majors adopted by women from the 1970s on. The percentage of women majoring in education declined beginning in the 1970s;[citation needed] education was once a popular major for women since it allowed them to step into and out of the labor force when they had children and when their children grew up to a reasonable age at which their mothers did not have to serve primarily as caretakers. Instead, majors such as business and management were on the rise in the 1970s, as women ventured into other fields that were once predominated by men.[citation needed] They experienced an expansion of their horizons and an alteration of what it meant to define their own identity. Women worked before they got married, and since women were marrying younger[citation needed] they were able to define themselves prior to a serious relationship.

The reasons for this big jump in the 1970s has been attributed by some scholars to widespread access to the birth control pill.[citation needed] While "the pill" was medically available in the 1960s, numerous laws restricted access to it. See, e.g., *Griswold v. Connecticut*, 381 U.S. 479 (1965) (overturning a Connecticut statute barring access to contraceptives) and *Eisenstadt v. Baird*, 405 U.S. 438 (1972) (establishing the right of unmarried people to access contraception). By the 1970s, the age of majority had been lowered from 21 to 18 in the United States, largely as a consequence of the Vietnam War; this also affected women's right to effect their own medical decisions. Since it had now become socially acceptable to postpone pregnancy even while married women had the luxury of thinking about other things, like education and work. Also, due to electrification women's work around the house became easier leaving them with more time to be able to dedicate to school or work. Due to the multiplier effect, even if some women were not blessed with access to the pill or electrification, many followed by the example of the other women entering the work force for those reasons. The Quiet Revolution is called such because it was not a "big bang" revolution; rather, it happened and is continuing to happen gradually.

Women in decision making

Female decision-makers from around Europe are organized in several national and European wide networks. The networks aim to promote women in decision-making positions in politics and the economy across Europe. These networks were founded in the 1980s and are often very different from the "service clubs" founded in the early days of the century, like Soroptimist and Zontas.

"Women in Management" is about women in business in usually male-dominated areas. Their motivation, their ideas and leadership styles and their ability to enter into leadership positions is the subject of most of the different networks.

As of 2009, women represented 20.9% of parliament in Europe (both houses) and 18.4% world average.

As of 2009, 90 women serve in the U.S. Congress: 17 women serve in the Senate, and 73 women serve in the House.

In the private sector, men still represent 9 out of 10 board members in European blue-chip companies, The discrepancy is widest at the very top: only 3% of these companies have a woman presiding over the highest decision-making body.[citation needed]

List of members of the European Network of Women in Decision-making in Politics and the Economy:

- Committee of Women Elected Representatives of Local and Regional Authorities (Council of European Municipalities and Regions)
- BPW Europe, Business and Professional Women – Europe
- Association of Organisations of Mediterranean Businesswomen
- Eurochambres Women's Network
- European Platform of Women Scientists
- Network of Parliamentary Committees for Equal Opportunities for Women and Men in the European Union
- European Network to Promote Women's Entrepreneurship
- European women's lobby
- European Women's Lawyers Association
- CEE Network for Gender Issues
- European Women Inventors and Innovators Network
- European Women's Management Development International Network, EWMD
- Femanet - Eurocadres
- European Professional Women's Network, EPWN
- Women's Forum for the Economy and the Society

The EU Commission has created a platform for all these networks. It also funded the Women to the Top program in 2003-2005 to bring more women into top management.

Some organizations have been created to promote the presence of women in top responsibilities, in politics and business. One example is EWMD European women's Management Development (cited above), a European and international network of individual and corporate members, drawn from professional organisations. Members are from all areas of business, education, politics and culture.

Women who are born into the upper class rather than the middle or lower class have a much better chance at holding higher positions of power in the work force if they choose to enter it.

Barriers to equal participation

As gender roles have followed the formation of agricultural and then industrial societies, newly developed professions and fields of occupation have been frequently inflected by gender. Some examples of the ways in which gender affects a field include:

- Prohibitions or restrictions on members of a particular gender entering a field or studying a field;
- Discrimination within a field, including wage, management, and prestige hierarchies;
- Expectation that mothers, rather than fathers, should be the primary childcare providers.

Note that these gender restrictions may not be universal in time and place, and that they operate to restrict both men and women. However, in practice, norms and laws have historically restricted women's access to particular occupations; civil rights laws and cases have thus primarily focused on equal access to and participation by *women* in the workforce. These barriers may also be manifested in hidden bias and by means of many micro-inequities.

Access to education

A number of occupations became "professionalized" through the 19th and 20th centuries, gaining regulatory bodies, and passing laws or regulations requiring particular higher educational requirements. As women's access to higher education was often limited, this effectively restricted women's participation in these professionalizing occupations. For instance, women were completely forbidden access to Cambridge University until 1868, and were encumbered with a variety of restrictions until 1987 when the university adopted an equal opportunity policy. Numerous other institutions in the United States and Western Europe began opening their doors to women over the same period of time, but access to higher education remains a significant barrier to women's full participation in the workforce in developing countries. Even where access to higher education is formally available, women's access to the full range of occupational choices is significantly limited where access to primary education is limited through social custom.

Access to capital

Women's access to occupations requiring capital outlays is also hindered by their unequal access (statistically) to capital; this affects occupations such as entrepreneur and small business owner, farm ownership, and investor. Numerous microloan programs attempt to redress this imbalance, targeting women for loans or grants to establish start-up businesses or farms, having determined that aid targeted to women can disproportionately benefit a nation's economy. While research has shown that women cultivate more than half the world's food — in sub-Saharan Africa and the Caribbean, women are responsible for up to 80% of food production — most such work is family subsistence labor, and often the family property is legally owned by the men in the family.

Discrimination within occupations

See also: Wage gap, Glass ceiling, and Sexual harassment

The idea that men and women are naturally suited for different occupations is known as horizontal segregation.

Statistical discrimination in the workplace is unintentional discrimination based on the presumed probability that a worker will or will not remain with the company for a long period of time. Specific to women, since employers believe that women are more likely to drop out of the labor force to have kids, or work part time while they are raising kids, this tends to hurt their chances for job advancement. They are passed up for promotions because of the possibility that they may leave, and are in some cases placed in positions with little opportunity for upward mobility to begin with based on these same stereotypes.

Women earn less money that men.

Network Discrimination

Part of the problem keeping women out of the highest paying, most prestigious positions is that they have historically not held these positions. As a result, recruiters for these high-status jobs are predominantly white males, and tend to hire similar people in their networks. Their networks are made up of mostly white males from the same socio-economic status, which helps perpetuate their over-representation in the best jobs.

Actions and Inactions of Women Themselves

Through a process known as employee clustering, employees tend to be grouped throughout the workplace both spatially and socially with those of a similar status job. Women are no exception and tend to be grouped with other women making comparable amounts of money. They compare wages with the women around them and believe their salaries are fair because they are average. Some women are content with their lack of wage equality with men in the same positions because they are unaware of just how vast the inequality is.

Furthermore, women as a whole tend to be less assertive and confrontational. One of the factors contributing to the unfair proportion of raises going to men is the simple fact that men tend to ask for raises more often than women, and are more aggressive when doing so.

Gender and women's history in particular occupations

Occupational Dissimilarity Index

Choice of occupation is considered to be one of the key factors contributing to the male-female wage differential. In other words, careers with a majority of female employees tend to pay less than careers that employ a majority of males. This is different from direct wage discrimination within occupations, as males in the female dominated professions will also make lower than average wages and the women in the male dominated occupations usually make higher than average wages. The occupational dissimilarity index is a measure from 0 to 100; it measures the percent of laborers that would need to be rearranged into a job typically done by the opposite sex in order for the wage differential to disappear. In 1960, the dissimilarity index in America was measured at 62. It has dropped since then, but at 47 in 2000, is still one of the highest of any developed nation.,

Womens participation in different occupations

below are a list of encyclopedia article links detailing women's historical involvement in various occupations.

- Sciences - See generally Women in science and List of female scientists
    - Women in computing (see also Women in the Information Age research project)
    - Women in engineering
    - Women in geology
    - List of female mathematicians
- Medical professions - See generally Women in medicine
- Legal professions - See generally Women in the United States judiciary

Though women comprise approximately half of the student body of American law schools, they represent only 17% of partners at major law firms and less than a quarter of tenured law professors. Similarly, on the national level, we have had only one female U.S. Attorney General, three female Secretaries of State, two women Supreme Court Justices, and one acting Solicitor General.

- Arts, writing, media, sports and entertainment
    - Women artists (visual arts)
    - Women Surrealists
    - Performing arts
        - Vulcana Women's Circus (organization for women in the circus)
    - Writing
        - Women's writing in English
        - Women in journalism and media professions
        - List of female rhetoricians
        - List of early-modern women playwrights (UK)
        - List of female poets
    - Film
        - List of female directors
        - Women's cinema (discusses women screenwriters & directors)
    - Music
        - Female composers in the United States during the 20th century
        - Women composers of Catholic music
        - List of female composers
        - List of female composers by name
        - List of female film score composers
    - Sports
        - Women's professional sports

- Women's sports and browse the category
- Humanities:
  - Women in philosophy and List of female philosophers
- Crime: Women in piracy
- Government: Women in politics
- Military:
  - Women in the military
  - Women in the military by country, in Europe, and in the Americas
  - History of women in the military; Timeline of women in ancient warfare; Timeline of Women in Medieval warfare
  - List of women warriors in folklore, literature, and popular culture
  - Category:Female military personnel;
  - Women's Land Army;
  - Category:Female wartime spies

Gender Inequality In the Different Social Classes

In the last 50 years we have experienced great changes toward gender equality in America. With the feminist movement of the 1960s, women began to enter the workforce in great numbers. Women had also had high labor market participation during World War II as so many male soldiers were away, women had to take up jobs to support their family and keep their local economy on track. Many of these women dropped right back out of the labor force when the men returned home from war to raise children born in the generation of the baby boomers. In the late 1960s when women began entering the labor force in record numbers, they were entering in addition to all of the men, as opposed to substituting for men during the war. This dynamic shift from the one-earner household to the two-earner household dramatically changed the socioeconomic class system of this country.

Effects of Women in the Workforce on the Middle and Upper Classes

The addition of women into the workforce was one of the key factors that has decreased social mobility over the last 50 years. Female children of the middle and upper classes had increased access to higher education, and thanks to job equality, were able to attain higher-paying and higher-prestige jobs than ever before. Due to the dramatic increase in availability of birth control, these high status women were able to delay marriage and child-bearing until they had completed their education and advanced their careers to their desired positions. In 2001, the survey on sexual harassment at workplace conducted by women's nonprofit organisation Sakshi among 2,410 respondents in government and non-government sectors, in five States recorded 53 per cent saying that both sexes don't get equal opportunities, 50 per cent women are treated unfairly by employers and co-workers, 59 per cent have heard sexist remarks or jokes, 32 per cent have been exposed to pornography or literature degrading women.

In comparison with other sectors, IT organisations may be offering equal salaries to women and the density of women in technology companies may be relatively high but this does not necessarily ensure a level playing field. For example Microsoft (US) was sued because of the conduct of one of its supervisors over e-mail. The supervisor allegedly made sexually offensive comments via e-mail, such as referring to himself as "president of the amateur gynecology club." He also allegedly referred to the plaintiff as the "Spandex Queen. E-harassment is not the sole form of harassment. In 1999, Juno Online faced two separate suits from former employees who alleged that they were told that they would be fired if they broke off their ongoing relationships with senior executives. Pseudo Programs, a Manhattan-based Internet TV network, was sued in January 2000 after male employees referred to female employees as "bimbos" and forced them to look at sexually explicit material on the Internet. In India HR managers admit that women are discriminated against for senior Board positions and pregnant women are rarely given jobs but only in private. Recently a sexual harassment suit against a senior member shocked the Indian IT sector.

Recognising the invisible nature of power structures that marginalise women at the workplace, the Supreme Court in the landmark Vaishaka versus High Court of Rajasthan (1997) identified sexual harassment as violative of the women's right to equality in the workplace and enlarged the ambit of its definition. The judgment equates a hostile work environment on the same plane as a direct request for sexual favours. To quote: "Sexual harassment includes such unwelcome sexually determined behaviour (whether directly or by implication) as: physical contact and advances; a demand or request for sexual favours; sexually coloured remarks; showing pornography; any other unwelcome physical, verbal or non-verbal conduct of sexual nature". The judgement mandates appropriate work conditions should be provided for work, leisure, health, and hygiene to further ensure that there is no hostile environment towards women at the workplace and no woman employee should have reasonable grounds to believe that she is disadvantaged in connection with her employment.

This law thus squarely shifts the onus onto the employer to ensure employee safety but most mid-sized Indian service technology companies are yet to enact sexual harassment policies. Admits K Chandan, an advocate from Chandan Associates, "I have a few IT clients. When I point to the need for a sexual harassment policy, most tend to overlook or ignore it. Its not high on the agenda." An HR Manager of India's premier technology companies rues: "I am going to use the recent case to push the policy through. Earlier the draft proposal was rejected by the company." Yet another HR manager from a flagship company of India's leading business house, oblivious to the irony of her statement, admitted that the company had a grievance redressal mechanism but no sexual harassment policy in place. The lax attitudes transgress the Supreme Court judgment wherein the Court not only defined sexual harassment, but also laid down a code of conduct for workplaces to prevent and punish it, "Employers or other responsible authorities in public or private sectors must comply with the following guidelines: Express prohibition of sexual harassment should be notified and circulated; private employers should include prohibition of sexual harassment in the standing orders under the Industrial Employment (Standing Orders) Act, 1946." As for the complaint procedure, not less than half of its members should be women. The complaint committee should include an NGO or other organisation that is familiar with the issue of sexual harassment. When the offence amounts to misconduct under service rules, appropriate disciplinary action should be initiated. When such conduct amounts to an offence under the Indian Penal Code, the employer shall initiate action by making a complaint with the appropriate authority. However, the survey by Sakshi revealed 58 per cent of women were not aware of the Supreme Court guidelines on the subject. A random survey by AssureConsulting.com among hundred employees working in the IT industry revealed startling results: Less than 10 per cent were familiar with the law or the company's sexual harassment policy. Surprisingly, certain HR managers were also ignorant of the Supreme Court guidelines or the Draft Bill by the National Commission of Women against sexual harassment at the workplace.

Not surprisingly many cases go unreported. However given the complexities involved, company policy is the first step and cannot wish away the problem. Says Savita HR Manager at Icelerate Technologies, "We have a sexual harassment policy that is circulated among employees. Also the company will not tolerate any case that comes to its notice. But the man at home is no different from the person at the office," thus implying the social mindset that discriminates against women is responsible for the problem. Considering sexual censorship and conservative social attitudes emphasising " woman's purity," the victim dare not draw attention for fear of being branded a woman with "loose morals". Women would rather brush away the problem or leave jobs quietly rather than speak up, even in organisations that have a zero tolerance policy. Says Chandan, "I do not have exact statistics but from my experience as an advocate one in 1,500 cases are reported." The problem cannot be resolved till more women speak up but the social set-up browbeats women into silence. The social stigma against the victim and the prolonged litigation process for justice thwarts most women from raising their voice. Purports K Chandan "It may take between three and five years to settle a case, and in a situation where the harassment is covert, evidence is hard to gather and there is no guarantee that the ruling would be in favour of the victim. In one of the rare cases I handled a Country Manager was accused and the plaintiff opted for an out of court settlement."

The dice is, thus, heavily loaded against women. Claims of new age companies of creating liberal and egalitarian workplaces are under serious examination. Companies can come clear by adopting a zero tolerance policy against sexism of any form. Probably the recent publicised case may just about drive companies to do so.

Effects of Women in the Workforce on the Working and Lower Classes

While middle and upper class women benefited from entering the workforce and the feminism movement, working and lower class women suffered. Women in lower wage jobs are more likely to be subject to wage discrimination. They are more likely to bring home far less than their male counterparts with equal job status, and get far less help with housework from their husbands than the high-earning women. Women with low educational attainment entering the workforce in mass quantity lowered earnings for some men, as the women brought about a lot more job competition. The lowered relative earnings of the men and increase in birth control made marriage prospects harder for lower income women.

For the first time in the history of this country, there were distinctive socioeconomic stratification among women as there has been among men for centuries. This deepened the inequality between the upper/middle and lower/working classes. Prior to the feminist movement, the socioeconomic status of a family was based almost solely on the husband/father's occupation. Women who were now attaining high status jobs were attractive partners to men with high status jobs, so the high earners married the high earners and the low earners married the low earners. In other words, the rich got richer and the poor stayed the same, and have had increased difficulty competing in the economy.

References

History of women in workforce; see also women's studies, gender studies, and women's history

- *Challenging Professions: Historical and Contemporary Perspectives on Women's Professional Work* by Elizabeth Smyth, Sandra Acker, Paula Bourne, and Alison Prentice
- *English women enter the professions* by Nellie Alden Franz (1965)
- *Black Women and White Women in the Professions: Occupational Segregation by Race and Gender, 1960-1980* (Perspectives on Gender) by N. Sokoloff (1992)
- *Unequal Colleagues: The Entrance of Women into the Professions, 1890-1940* (Douglass Series on Women's Lives and the Meaning of Gender) by Penina Migdal Glazer and Miriam Slater
- *Beyond Her Sphere: Women and the Professions in American History* by Barbara J. Harris
- "Challenging Professions: Historical and Contemporary Perspectives on Women's Professional Work" (Book Reviews) Pamela Sugiman in *Relations Industrielles/Industrial Relations*
- *Victorian Working Women: A historical and literary study of women in British industries and professions 1832-1850* (Economic History (Routledge)) by Wanda F. Neff
- *Colonial women of affairs,: A study of women in business and the professions in America before 1776* by Elisabeth Anthony Dexter
- *What a Woman Ought to Be and to Do: Black Professional Women Workers during the Jim Crow Era* (Women in Culture and Society Series) by Stephanie J. Shaw
- *In Subordination: Professional Women, 1870-1970* by Mary Kinnear
- *Women Working in Nontraditional Fields References and Resources 1963-1988* (Women's Studies Series) by Carroll Wetzel Wilkinson

Social sciences and psychological perspectives; see also women's studies and gender studies

- Suhail Ahmad, *Women in profession: A comparative study of Hindu and Muslim women*
- Ella L. J. Edmondson Bell and Stella M. Nkomo, *Our Separate Ways: Black and White Women and the Struggle for Professional Identity*

- Julia Evetts, *Women and Career: Themes and Issues in Advanced Industrial Societies* (Longman Sociology Series)
- Patricia N. Feulner, *Women in the Professions: A Social-Psychological Study*
- Linda S. Fidell and John D. DeLamater, *Women in the Professions*
- Clara Greed, *Surveying Sisters: Women in a Traditional Male Profession*
- Jerry Jacobs, *Professional Women at Work: Interactions, Tacit Understandings, and the Non-Trivial Nature of Trivia in Bureaucratic Settings*
- Edith J. Morley, *Women Workers in Seven Professions*
- Xiomara Santamarina, *Belabored Professions: Narratives of African American Working Womanhood*
- Janet Skarbek, *Planning Your Future: A Guide for Professional Women*
- Elizabeth Smyth, Sandra Acker, Paula Bourne, and Alison Prentice, *Challenging Professions: Historical and Contemporary Perspectives on Women's Professional Work*
- Nancy C. Talley-Ross, *Jagged Edges: Black Professional Women in White Male Worlds* (Studies in African and African-American Culture, Vol 7) (1995)
- Joyce Tang and Earl Smith, *Women and Minorities in American Professions* (S U N Y Series on the New Inequalities)
- Anne Witz, "Patriarchy and Professions: The Gendered Politics of Occupational Closure", *Sociology*, 24.4, 1990, pp. 675–690. See Sage Publications [1].
- Anne Witz, *Professions and Patriarchy* (International Library of Sociology) (1992)

Work and family demands/support for women

- Terri Apter, *Working Women Don't Have Wives: Professional Success in the 1990s*
- Sian Griffiths, *Beyond the Glass Ceiling: Forty Women Whose Ideas Shape the Modern World* (Women's Studies)
- Linda Hantrais, *Managing Professional and Family Life: A Comparative Study of British and French Women*
- Deborah J. Swiss and Judith P. Walker, *Women and the Work/Family Dilemma: How Today's Professional Women Are Finding Solutions*
- Alice M. Yohalem, *The Careers of Professional Women: Commitment and Conflict*

Workplace discrimination based on gender

- The Commission on Women in the Profession, *Sex-Based Harassment, 2nd Edition: Workplace Policies for the Legal Profession*
- Sylvia Ann Hewlett, *Off-ramps and On-ramps: Keeping Talented Women on the Road to Success*
- Karen Maschke, *The Employment Context* (Gender and American Law: The Impact of the Law on the Lives of Women)
- Evelyn Murphy and E.J. Graff, *Getting Even: Why Women Don't Get Paid Like Men—And What to Do About It* (2006)

Mentoring and "old-boys/old-girls networks"

- Nancy W. Collins, *Professional Women and Their Mentors: A Practical Guide to Mentoring for the Woman Who Wants to Get Ahead*
- Carolyn S. Duff, *Learning From Other Women: How to Benefit From the Knowledge, Wisdom, and Experience of Female Mentors*
- Joan Jeruchim, *Women, Mentors, and Success*
- Peggy A. Pritchard, *Success Strategies for Women in Science: A Portable Mentor* (Continuing Professional Development Series)

Arts and literature studies on women in the workforce

- Carmen Rose Marshall, *Black Professional Women in Recent American Fiction*

Professional areas

Teaching, librarianship, and university professions

- Maenette K. P. Benham and Joanne Cooper, *Let My Spirit Soar!: Narratives of Diverse Women in School Leadership (1-Off)*
- Roger Blanpain and Ann Numhauser-Henning, *Women in Academia and Equality Law: Aiming High, Falling Short? Denmark, France, Germany, Hungary, Italy, the Netherlands, Sweden, United Kingdom* (Bulletin of Comparative Labour Relations)
- S. A. L. Cavanagh, The Gender of Professionalism and Occupational Closure: the management of tenure-related disputes by the 'Federation of Women Teachers' Associations of Ontario' 1918-1949, Gender and Education, 15.1, March 2003, pp. 39–57. See Routledge [2].
- Regina Cortina and Sonsoles San Roman, *Women and Teaching: Global Perspectives on the Feminization of a Profession*
- Nancy Hoffman, *Woman's "True" Profession*, 2nd ed. (1982, 2nd ed.) ("classic history of women and the teaching profession in the United States")
- Julia Kwong, Ma Wanhua, and Wanhua Ma, *Chinese Women and the Teaching Profession*
- See also Category:Female academics

Philosophy

- See also Women in philosophy and Category:Women philosophers

Social sciences

- Kathleen Bowman and Larry Soule, *New Women in Social Sciences* (1980)
- Lynn McDonald, *The Women Founders of the Social Sciences* (1994)
- See also: Category:Women social scientists

Social sciences – Anthropology

- Barbara A. Babcock and Nancy J. Parezo, *Daughters of the Desert: Women Anthropologists and the Native American Southwest, 1880-1980* (1988)

- Ruth Behar and Deborah A. Gordon, *Women Writing Culture* (1996)
- Maria G. Cattell and Marjorie M. Schweitzer, *Women in Anthropology: Autobiographical Narratives and Social History* (2006)
- Ute D. Gacs, Aisha Khan, Jerrie McIntyre, and Ruth Weinberg, *Women Anthropologists: Selected Biographies* (1989); *Women Anthropologists: A Biographical Dictionary* (1988)
- Nancy Parezo, *Hidden Scholars: Women Anthropologists and the Native American* (1993)

Social sciences – Archaeology

- Cheryl Claassen, *Women in Archaeology* (1994)
- Margarita Diaz-Andreu and Marie Louise Stig Sorensen, *Excavating Women: A History of Women in European Archaeology* (1998; 2007)
- Getzel M. Cohen and Martha Sharp Joukowsky, editors, *Breaking Ground: Pioneering Women Archaeologists* (2004)
- Nancy Marie White, Lynne P. Sullivan, and Rochelle A. Marrinan, *Grit-Tempered: Early Women Archaeologists in Southeastern United States* (2001)

Social sciences – History

- Eileen Boris and Nupur Chaudhuri, *Voices of Women Historians: The Personal, the Political, the Professional* (1999)
- Jennifer Scanlon and Shaaron Cosner, *American Women Historians, 1700s-1990s: A Biographical Dictionary* (1996)
- Nadia Smith, *A "Manly Study"?: Irish Women Historians, 1868-1949* (2007)
- Deborah Gray White, *Telling Histories: Black Women Historians in the Ivory Tower* (forthcoming 2008)
- Southern Association for Women Historians [3]

Social sciences – Linguistics

- Davison, *The Cornell Lectures: Women in the Linguistics Profession*

"STEM" fields (science, technology, engineering, and maths); see also women in science

- Violet B. Haas and Carolyn C. Perrucci, *Women in Scientific and Engineering Professions* (Women and Culture Series)
- Patricia Clark Kenschaft, *Change Is Possible: Stories of Women and Minorities in Mathematics*
- J A Mattfeld, *Women & the Scientific Professions*
- Jacquelyn A. Mattfeld and Carol E. Van Aken, *Women and the Scientific Professions: The MIT Symposium on American Women in Science and Engineering* (1964 symposium; 1976 publication)
- Karen Mahony & Brett Van Toen, Mathematical Formalism as a Means of Occupational Closure in Computing—Why "Hard" Computing Tends to Exclude Women, Gender and Education, 2.3, 1990, pp. 319–31. See ERIC record. [4]

- Peggy A. Pritchard, *Success Strategies for Women in Science: A Portable Mentor* (Continuing Professional Development Series)
- Margaret W. Rossiter, *Women Scientists in America: Struggles and Strategies to 1940* (Women Scientists in America)
- Otha Richard Sullivan and Jim Haskins, *Black Stars: African American Women Scientists and Inventors*
- See also Category:Women engineers; Category:Women scientists
- See also List of pre-21st-century female scientists

Medical professions

- See Women in the medical professions and Category:Midwives

Legal professions

- Joan Brockman and Dorothy E. Chunn, "A new order of things": women's entry into the legal profession in British Columbia", *The Advocate*
- The Commission on Women in the Profession, *Visible Invisibility: Women of Color in Law Firms*
- The Commission on Women in the Profession, *Sex-Based Harassment, 2nd Edition: Workplace Policies for the Legal Profession*
- Hedda Garza, *Barred from the Bar: A History of Women in the Legal Profession* (Women Then—Women Now)
- Jean Mckenzie Leiper, *Bar Codes: Women in the Legal Profession*
- Sheila McIntyre and Elizabeth Sheehy, *Calling for Change: Women, Law, and the Legal Profession*
- Mary Jane Mossman, *The First Women Lawyers: A Comparative Study of Gender, Law And the Legal Professions*
- Rebecca Mae Salokar and Mary L. Volcansek, *Women in Law: A Bio-Bibliographical Sourcebook*
- Ulrike Schultz and Gisela Shaw, *Women in the World's Legal Professions* (Onati International Series in Law and Society)
- Lisa Sherman, Jill Schecter, and Deborah Turchiano, *Sisters-In-Law: an Uncensored Guide for Women Practicing Law in the real world*
- See Women in the U.S. Judiciary and categories Category:Women judges and Category:Female lawyers

Religious professions

- Stanley J. Grenz and Denise Muir Kjesbo, *Women in the Church: A Biblical Theology of Women in Ministry*
- Lenore Friedman, *Meetings with Remarkable Women: Buddhist Teachers in America*
- See also Category:Female religious leaders and Category:Nuns and List of female mystics

Helping professions (social work, childcare, eldercare, etc.)

- Ski Hunter, Sandra Stone Sundel, and Martin Sundel, *Women at Midlife: Life Experiences and Implications for the Helping Professions*
- Linda Reeser, Linda Cherrey, and Irwin Epstein, *Professionalization and Activism in Social Work* (1990) (covers gender as part of history of professionalization), Columbia University Press, ISBN 0231067887
- Sarah Stage and Virginia B. Vincenti, editors, *Rethinking Home Economics: Women and the History of a Profession*
- See also Category:Governesses

Journalism and media professions

- See Women in journalism and media professions

Architecture and design

- *Designing for Diversity: Gender, Race, and Ethnicity in the Architectural Profession* by Kathryn H. Anthony
- *The First American Women Architects* by Sarah Allaback (forthcoming 2008)
- See also Category:Women architects

Arts and literature; see also Women's writing in English and Women artists

- Margaret Barlow, *Women Artists*
- Whitney Chadwick, *Women Artists and the Surrealist Movement*
- Liz Rideal, Whitney Chadwick, and Frances Borzello, *Mirror Mirror: Self-Portraits by Women Artists*
- Jo Franceschina, *Women and the Profession of Theater, 1810-1860*
- National Geographic Society, *Women Photographers at National Geographic*
- Laura R. Prieto, *At Home in the Studio: The Professionalization of Women Artists in America*
- See also Category:Women artists, Category:Female dancers, Category:Female choreographers, Category:Women comedians, Category:Women comics artists, Category:Women composers, Category:Female film directors, Category:Female singers

Entertainment and modeling

- Ann Cvetkovich, "Fierce Pussies and Lesbian Avengers: Dyke Activism Meets Celebrity Culture" (images of female models merging infiltrating other cultures)
- Michael Gross, *Model: The Ugly Business of Beautiful Women* (2003) (history of female modeling);
- Ian Halperin, *Shut Up and Smile: Supermodels, the Dark Side* (1999)
- Nancy Hellmich, "Do thin models warp girls' body image?", *USA Today*, Sept. 26, 2006
- Jennifer Melocco, "Ban on Stick-Thin Models Illegal", *Daily Telegraph*, Feb. 16, 2007
- Barbara Summers, *Black and Beautiful: How Women of Color Changed the Fashion Industry* (racism within modeling)
- Barbara Summers, *Skin Deep: Inside the World of Black Fashion Models* (1999)

- Naomi Wolf, *The Beauty Myth: How Images of Beauty Are Used Against Women* (1991)
- See also Category:Female models, Category:Female pornographic film actors, Category:Beauty pageant contestants

Explorers, navigators, travelers, settlers

- Joanna Stratton, *Pioneer Women*
- David Cordingly, *Seafaring Women: Adventures of Pirate Queens, Female Stowaways, and Sailors' Wives*
- See also Category:Female explorers, Category:Female astronauts, Category:Female aviators

Sports and athletics

- Karra Porter, *Mad Seasons: The Story of the First Women's Professional Basketball League, 1978-1981*
- See also: Category:Sportswomen, Category:Female athletes, Category:Female dancers, Category:Female bullfighters,

Business and leadership

- Roger E. Axtell, Tami Briggs, Margaret Corcoran, and Mary Beth Lamb, *Do's and Taboos Around the World for Women in Business*
- Douglas Branson, *No Seat at the Table: How Corporate Governance and Law Keep Women Out of the Boardroom*
- Lin Coughlin, Ellen Wingard, and Keith Hollihan, *Enlightened Power: How Women are Transforming the Practice of Leadership*
- Harvard Business School Press, editors, *Harvard Business Review on Women in Business*
- S. N. Kim, "Racialized gendering of the accountancy profession: toward an understanding of Chinese women's experiences in accountancy in New Zealand" in *Critical Perspectives on Accounting*
- Deborah Rhode, *The Difference ""Difference"" Makes: Women and Leadership* (2002)
- Judy B. Rosener, *America's Competitive Secret: Women Managers*
- Robert E. Seiler, *Women in the Accounting Profession* (1986)
- See also Category:Women in business

European Union initiatives and information

- Report"Women and men in decision-making 2007 – analysis of the situation and trends" [5]
- Database on women in decision-making [6]
- Commission's Roadmap for Equality between women and men (2006-2010) [7]

Public policy and governmental occupations

- See also List of the first female holders of political office in Europe and List of the first female holders of political offices

- See also Women in politics and categories Category:Female diplomats, Category:Female civil servants, Category:Women sheriffs, Category:Female police officers, Category:Women in politics

Military professions

- See: History of women in the military; Women's Land Army; Category:Female military personnel; Category:Female wartime spies

Criminal occupations

See Women in crime and Category:Female pirates

See also
- Rosie the Riveter
- Women's history
- Women's studies
- Gender studies
- Workplace discrimination, Occupational sexism, and Glass ceiling
- Labor history
- Educational Inequality
- Timeline of women's rights (other than voting)

Rosie

Rosie the Riveter

Rosie the Riveter is a cultural icon of the United States, representing the American women who worked in factories during World War II, many of whom worked in the manufacturing plants that produced munitions and war supplies. These women sometimes took entirely new jobs replacing the male workers who were in the military. The character is considered a feminist icon in the US.

History

The term **"Rosie the Riveter"** was first used in 1942 in a song of the same name written by Redd Evans and John Jacob Loeb. The song was recorded by numerous artists, including the popular big band leader Kay Kyser, and became a national hit. The song portrays "Rosie" as a tireless assembly line worker, doing her part to help the American war effort:

> All the day long,
> Whether rain or shine
> She's part of the assembly line.
> She's making history,
> Working for victory
> Rosie the Riveter

Although real-life Rosie the Riveters took on male dominated trades during WWII, women were expected to return to their everyday housework once men returned from the war. Government campaigns targeting women were addressed solely at housewives, perhaps because already employed women would move to the higher-paid "essential" jobs on their own. Most women opted to do this. Later many women chose to return to traditional work such as clerical or administration positions. However, some of these women continued working in the factories.

A real-life "Rosie" at work

The individual who was the inspiration for the song was Rosalind P. Walter, who "came from old money and worked on the night shift building the F4U Corsair fighter." Later in life Walter was a philanthropist, a board member of the WNET public television station in New York and an early and long-time supporter of the Charlie Rose interview show.

Rosie the Riveter became most closely associated with another real woman, Rose Will Monroe, who was born in Pulaski County, Kentucky in 1920 and moved to Michigan during World War II. She worked as a riveter at the Willow Run Aircraft Factory in Ypsilanti, Michigan, building B-29 and B-24 bombers for the U.S. Army Air Forces. Monroe achieved her dream of piloting a plane when she was in her 50's and her love of flying resulted in an accident that contributed to her death 19 years later. Monroe was asked to star in a promotional film about the war effort at home. The song "Rosie the Riveter" was popular at the time, and Monroe happened to best fit the description of the worker depicted in the song. Rosie went on to become perhaps the most widely recognized icon of that era. The films and posters she appeared in were used to encourage women to go to work in support of the war effort.

Man and woman riveting team working on the cockpit shell of a C-47 aircraft at the plant of North American Aviation. Office of War Information photo by Alfred T. Palmer, 1942.

According to the *Encyclopedia of American Economic History*, "Rosie the Riveter" inspired a social movement that increased the number of working American women to 20 million by 1944, a 57% increase from 1940.[*citation needed*] Although the image of "Rosie the Riveter" reflected the industrial work of welders and riveters during World War II, the majority of working women filled non-factory positions in every sector of the economy.What unified the experiences of these women was that they proved to themselves (and the country) that they could do a "man's job" and could do it well. In 1942, just between the months of January and July, the estimates of the proportion of jobs that would be "acceptable" for women was raised by employers from 29 to 85%.[*citation needed*] African American women were some of those most affected by the need for women workers. It has been said that it was the process of whites working along blacks during the time that encouraged a breaking down of social barriers and a healthy recognition of diversity African-Americans were able to lay the groundwork for the postwar civil rights revolution by equating segregation with Nazi white supremacist ideology.

Conditions were sometimes harsh and pay was not always equal—the average man working in a wartime plant was paid $54.65 per week, while women were paid about $50. Nonetheless, women quickly responded to Rosie the Riveter, who convinced them that they had a patriotic duty to enter the workforce. Some claim that she forever opened the work force for women, but others dispute that point, noting that many women were discharged after the war and their jobs were given to returning servicemen.[citation needed] These critics claim that when peace returned, few women returned to their wartime positions and instead resumed domestic vocations or transferred into sex-typed occupations such as clerical and service work. For some, World War II represented a major turning point for women as they eagerly supported the war effort, while other historians emphasize that the changes were temporary and that immediately after the war was over, women were expected to return to traditional roles of wives and mothers, and finally, a third group has emphasized how the long-range significance of the changes brought about by the war provided the foundation for the contemporary woman's movement. Leila J. Rupp in her study of World War II wrote "For the first time, the working woman dominated the public image. Women were riveting housewives in slacks, not mother, domestic beings, or civilizers."

After the war, the "Rosies" and the generations that followed them knew that working in the factories was in fact a possibility for women, even though they did not reenter the job market in such large proportions again until the 1970s. By that time factory employment was in decline all over the country.[citation needed]

On October 14, 2000, the Rosie the Riveter/World War II Home Front National Historical Park was opened in Richmond, California, site of four Kaiser shipyards, where thousands of "Rosies" from around the country worked (although ships at the Kaiser yards were not riveted, but rather welded). Over 200 former Rosies attended the ceremony.

The documentary film *The Life and Times of Rosie the Riveter* addresses the history of Rosie.

The image most iconically associated with Rosie is J. Howard Miller's famous poster for Westinghouse, titled *We Can Do It!*, which was modeled on the middle Michigan factory worker Geraldine Doyle in 1942, but this image was not actually intended to be Rosie the Riveter. Rosie the Riveter is a fictional character.

J. Howard Miller's "We Can Do It!", a classic rendition of Rosie the Riveter

Posters

Westinghouse Poster. "In 1942, Pittsburgh artist J. Howard Miller was hired by the Westinghouse Company's War Production Coordinating Committee to create a series of posters for the war effort. One of these posters became the famous "We Can Do It!" image — an image that in later years would also become "Rosie the Riveter," though not intended at its creation. Miller based his "We Can Do It!" poster on a United Press photograph taken of Michigan factory worker Geraldine Doyle. Its intent was to help recruit women to join the work force. At the time of the poster's release the name "Rosie" was not associated with the image. The poster — one of many in Miller's Westinghouse series — was not initially seen much beyond one Midwest Westinghouse factory where it was displayed for two weeks in February 1942. It was only later, around the 1970s and 1980s, that the Miller poster was rediscovered and became famous as 'Rosie The Riveter.'"

Saturday Evening Post. Norman Rockwell's image of "Rosie the Riveter" received mass distribution on the cover of the Saturday Evening Post in 1943. Rockwell's illustration features a brawny women named 'Rosie' taking her lunch break with a rivet gun on her lap and beneath her boot a copy of Hitler's manifesto, *Mein Kampf.*

Shirley Karp

In 1943-1945, Shirley Karp Dick (who was the original Rosie during 1939-1941) revived her role as Rosie the Riveter. She was paid $6 to model. Two of her most famous photos were of Rosie treading on a book written by Adolf Hitler, and of her in a U.S fighter (with another woman fueling up the plane). During her tenure as Rosie, Shirley was part of the movement that motivated over 11 million women to join in World War II, by doing the paperwork, making guns for soldiers, or doing other service in the war effort.

Shirley Karp died on January 15, 2009 at the age of 85; at the time she was the oldest living Rosie the Riveter model.

Homages

According to Penny Colman's *Rosie the Riveter*, there was also, very briefly, a "Wendy the Welder" based on Janet Doyle, a worker at the Kaiser Richmond Liberty Shipyards in California.

In the 1960s, Hollywood actress Jane Withers gained fame as "Josephine the Plumber," a character in a long-running and popular series of television commercials for "Comet" cleansing powder that lasted into the 1970s. This character was based on the original "Rosie" character and thus owes much to exemplary women's efforts in the traditional male workplace.

More recent cultural references include a character called "Rosie" in the video game *BioShock*, armed with a rivet gun. There's a DC Comics character called *Rosie The Riveter* [1], who wields a rivet gun as a weapon (and first appeared in Green Lantern vol. 2 #176 (May, 1984)). In the video game Fallout 3 there are billboards featuring "Rosies" assembling Atomic Bombs while drinking Nuka-Cola. A Rosie the Riveter action figurine is made by Accoutrements, although loosely based on Miller's anonymous poster. In the final bars at 3:06 of the *video* [2] track clock, in **Candyman**, by **Christina Aguilera**, which emulates the famous **Andrews Sisters** vocal harmonies of the WW-II era - while wearing a red bandanna and shot with the era's vintage **Technicolor** color processing scheme, Christina gives the famous "Rosie" pose, with fist-up, and right hand on biceps. Beyonce Knowles also uses the idea in her 2010 "Why Don't You Love Me?" Video. In June 2009 Crystal Bridges museum in Bentonville has acquired Norman Rockwell's iconic Rosie the Riveter painting for its permanent collection from a private collector. Country music singer Emma Jacob, on her album "Strong Like Me", accurately recreates the Rosie the Riveter image for the album's cover.

See also

- United States home front during World War II
- Women's roles in the World Wars
- Women's Land Army - British farm workers ("land girls")
- Woman's Land Army of America ("farmettes")
- Australian Women's Land Army
- Canary girl - British women working in munitions
- Ronnie the Bren Gun Girl - the Canadian equivalent
- Women in the workforce
- Greatest Generation

References

Sources

- Bornstein, Anna 'Dolly' Gillan. Woman Welder/ Shipbuilder in World War II. Winnie the Welder History Project. Schlesinger Library, Radcliffe College. February 16, 2005.
- Bourke-White, Margaret. "Women In Steel: They are Handling Tough Jobs In Heavy Industry". *Life*. August 9, 1943.
- Bowman, Constance. *Slacks and Calluses - Our Summer in a Bomber Factory*. Smithsonian Institution. Washington D.C. 1999.
- Cabanis, Helen. *Woman Riveter in World War II*. Rosie the Riveter Collection, Rose State College, Eastern Oklahoma Country Regional History. Center. [Rosie the Riveter Collection, Rose State College] March 16, 2003.
- Campbell, D'Ann. *Women at War with America: Private Lives ina Patriotic Era* (Harvard University Press: 1984)
- Hresko, Mary and Mary Vincher Shiner. *Women Workers in World War II* [1]. Wikipedia:Link rot May 21, 2001.
- Meacham, Clarice. *Woman Welder and Riveter during World War II*. Personal Interview. December 13, 2004.

- Regis, Margaret. *When Our Mothers Went to War: An Illustrated History of Women in World War II.* [1] Seattle: NavPublishing, 2008. ISBN 978-1-87732-05-0.
- "Rosie the Riveter" Redd Evans and John Jacob Loeb. Paramount Music Corporation, 1942.
- Ware, Susan. *Modern American Women A Documetary History.* McGraw-Hill:2002.184.
- Wise, Nancy Baker and Christy Wise. *A Mouthful of Rivets: Women at Work in World War II.* San Francisco: Jossey-Bass Publishers, 1994.

Further Reading
- William L. Bird, Jr. and Harry R. Rubenstein. *Design for Victory: World War II Posters on the American Home Front.* New York: Princeton Architectural Press, 1998.

External links
- Library of Congress Webcast [2]
- Rosie the Riveter World War II / Home Front National Historical Park [3]
- Regional Oral History Office / Rosie the Riveter / WWII American Homefront Project [8]
- American Rosie the Riveter Association [4]
- A Real-Life "Rosie the Riveter" [5]
- Another Real-Life "Rosie" from the Library of Congress' image set [6]
- "Rosie the Riveter" image is not the same as "We Can Do It!" [7]
- "Rosie the Riveter - We Can Do It! - Woven Image" [8]
- http://hypeshow.nasanu.com/index.php/result/index/keywords/The Life and Times of Rosie the Riveter movie
- Christina Aguilera in a "Rosie the Riveter" pose in the Candyman music video - see 3:06 on video track clock - playing at Youtube [2]
- Freeze-frame image of Christina Aguilera in a "Rosie the Riveter" pose from the Candyman music video [9]
- Oral history interview with Audrey Lyons, a "real life" Rosie, who worked in the Brooklyn shipyard during WWII [10] from the Veterans History Project at Central Connecticut State University
- Oral history interview with Mary Doyle Keefe, who modeled for Norman Rockwell's "Rosie the Riveter" painting [11] from the Veterans History Project at Central Connecticut State University

Willow Run Airport

Willow Run Airport (YIP)	
IATA: YIP – ICAO: KYIP	
Summary	
Airport type	Public
Operator	Wayne County Airport Authority
Location	Van Buren Charter Township and Ypsilanti Township
Hub for	{{{hub}}}
Elevation AMSL	716 ft / 218 m
Coordinates	42°14′16.539″N 83°31′49.472″W

Runways			
Direction	Length		Surface
	ft	m	
5L/23R	6,653	2,028	Paved
5R/23L	7,526	2,294	Paved
9/27	7,293	2,223	Paved
14/32	6,912	2,107	Paved

Willow Run Airport (IATA: **YIP**, ICAO: **KYIP**) is an airport located in Van Buren Charter Township and in Ypsilanti Township, near Ypsilanti, Michigan, that serves freight, corporate, and general aviation clients. No commercial passenger services are available at the airport. The airport has four runways (the fifth runway, 9R/27L, was recently closed and redesginated taxiway H), a continuously staffed FAA control tower, and US Customs operations. Willow Run Airport is one of two facilities operated by Wayne County Airport Authority, the other being Detroit Metropolitan Wayne County Airport, which replaced Willow Run as the major commercial airport for the region in the late 1960s. Major worldwide cargo airlines Kalitta Air and National Airlines are based at Willow Run Airport.

History

Willow Run Airport was built during World War II along with the Willow Run plant, where the Ford Motor Company produced
B-24 bombers for the US Government. Bomber production ceased at the plant after the war, and it was converted into a passenger terminal. Commercial passenger traffic was moved from Detroit City Airport, making Willow Run Detroit's primary airport.

In 1946 Warren Avis founded Avis Airlines Rent a Car Systems at Willow Run Airport. It was the first rental car operation at an airport location.

The Federal Government sold the airport to the University of Michigan in 1947 for $1.00. Terms of the sale required that the university operate the airport as a research facility, and the Michigan Aeronautical Research Center (later renamed Willow Run Research Center) was founded. For a time, the university housed part of its student population in the apartments previously used by plant workers.

In 1956, there were seven commercial passenger carriers operating out of Willow Run. Commercial service began to shift to the nearby Detroit Metro Airport during the late 1950s, and by 1967 it had ceased altogether.

In 1977, the University of Michigan sold the airport to Wayne County for $1.00.

The Yankee Air Museum opened on the airport grounds in 1981. A fire in October 2004 destroyed the museums building and most of its artifacts. The static display aircraft like the B-52 and other aircraft that were too large to be on display inside the hangar were undamaged. In 2005 the museum moved to the other side of the airport where they are rebuilding their displays and gathering more WWII memorabilia.

See also

- Detroit Metropolitan Wayne County Airport
- Michigan World War II Army Airfields
- Eastern Air Defense Force (Air Defense Command)
- 30th Air Division (United States)

References

- "Rad Lab History" [1]. Retrieved July 17, 2005.
- Olivia Murray. "Once Upon a Time in Willow Run" [2]. *Michigan Today*. Retrieved July 17, 2005.

External links

- Willow Run Airport [3]
- Resources for this airport:
    - AirNav airport information for KYIP [4]
    - ASN accident history for YIP [5]
    - FlightAware airport information [6] and live flight tracker [7]
    - NOAA/NWS latest weather observations [8]
    - SkyVector aeronautical chart for KYIP [9]
    - FAA current YIP delay information [10]

Richmond Shipyards

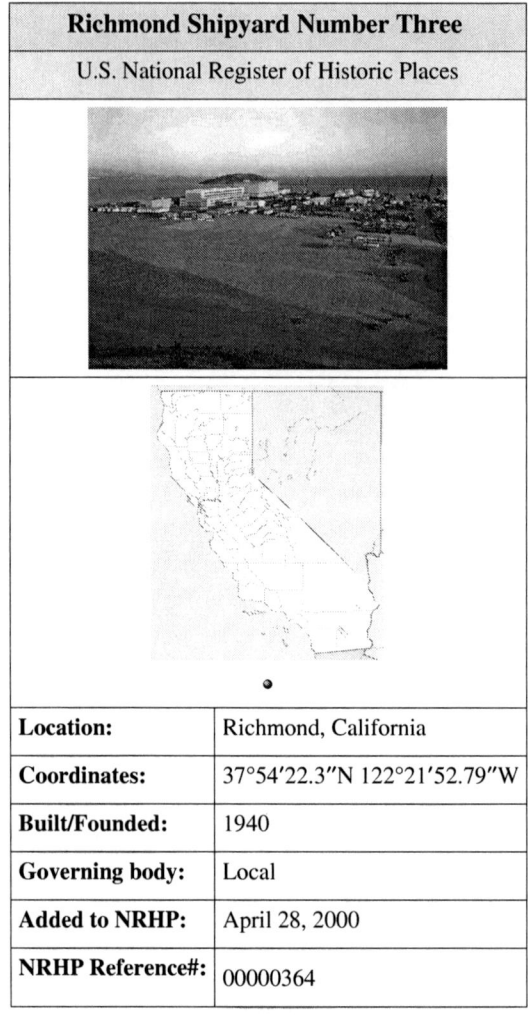

Richmond Shipyard Number Three	
U.S. National Register of Historic Places	
Location:	Richmond, California
Coordinates:	37°54′22.3″N 122°21′52.79″W
Built/Founded:	1940
Governing body:	Local
Added to NRHP:	April 28, 2000
NRHP Reference#:	00000364

The four **Richmond Shipyards**, located in the city of Richmond, California, United States, were run by Permanente Metals and part of the Kaiser Shipyards, and were responsible for constructing more ships during World War II than any other shipyard in the country. The shipyards are part of the Rosie the Riveter/World War II Home Front National Historical Park. The park's Rosie the Riveter memorial is located on the former grounds of Shipyard #2. Shipyard #3 is listed on the National Register of Historic Places.

Henry J. Kaiser had been building cargo ships for the U.S. Maritime Commission in the late 1930s. When orders for ships from the British government, already at war with Nazi Germany, allowed for growth, Kaiser established his first Richmond shipyard, beginning in December, 1940.

More than 747 vessels were built here in the four Richmond Kaiser Shipyards during World War II; a feat not equaled anywhere else in the world, before or since. These ships were completed in two-thirds the amount of time and at a quarter of the cost of the average of all other shipyards. The Liberty ship SS *Robert E. Peary* was assembled in less than five days as a part of a special competition among shipyards; but by 1944 it was only taking the astonishingly brief time of a little over two weeks to assemble a Liberty ship by standard methods.

Henry Kaiser and his workers applied mass assembly line techniques to building the ships. This production line technique, bringing pre-made parts together, moving them into place with huge cranes and having them welded together by "Rosies" (actually "Wendy the Welders" here in the shipyards), allowed unskilled laborers to do repetitive jobs requiring relatively little training to accomplish. This not only increased the speed of construction, but also the size of the mobilization effort, and in doing so, opened up jobs to women and minorities.

During WWII, thousands of men and women worked in this area every day, in very hazardous jobs. Actively recruited by Kaiser, they came from all over the United States to swell the population of Richmond from 20,000 to over 100,000 in three short years. For many of them, this was the first time they worked and earned money. It was the first time they were faced with the problems of being working parents -- finding day care and housing. Women and minorities entered the workforce in areas previously denied to them. However, they still faced unequal pay, were shunted off into "auxiliary" unions and still had to deal with day-to-day prejudice and inequities. During the war, there were labor strikes and sit-down work stoppages that eventually led to better conditions.

Many workers commuted from other parts of the Bay Area to the Kaiser Shipyards in Richmond by way of the Shipyard Railway, a temporary wartime railway which ran from a depot in Emeryville, California to a loop line serving all four of the shipyards, and utilizing cars of the local Key System.

The shipyard is currently closed to the public while safe methods of public access are developed. The SS *Red Oak Victory* is docked nearby.

References

This article incorporates public domain material [1] *from websites or documents of the National Park Service.*

External links

- Images and oral history transcripts describing the early days of the Richmond Shipyards [2], via Calisphere, California Digital Library.
- Permanente Metals Corporation - Kaiser Richmond CA Shipyards [3]

Rosie the Riveter/World War II Home Front National Historical Park

Rosie the Riveter/World War II Home Front National Historical Park	
U.S. National Register of Historic Places	
U.S. National Historical Park	
 J. Howard Miller's "We Can Do It!" poster, commonly associated with Rosie the Riveter.	
Location:	Shipyards of Richmond, Richmond, California
Area:	145 acres (59 ha)
Governing body:	National Park Service
Added to NRHP:	January 31, 2001
Designated NHP:	October 25, 2000
NRHP Reference#:	01000287

Rosie the Riveter/World War II Home Front National Historical Park is located in Richmond, California, near San Francisco. The park encompasses an array of historic properties in the city which were constructed during the 1940s to support America's entry into World War II.

The park is a "partnership park", meaning that no land or buildings are actually owned by the National Park Service, which only administers the park. This relatively new National Park was established in 2000 and is still under development. Bus tours of the park began in 2007 and were run by the city as the park has formed a unique partnership and is jointly administered by the National Parks Service and the city government.

Park attractions

During this initial developmental phase, the park has limited visitor services. A self guided auto tour with optional walking tour is available for downloading. In the summer of 2007 prelimentary bus tours were begun with a new guideless model, which instead filled half of the bus with residents who spoke of their experiences from the time to put what are otherwise everyday streets for residents into a greater historical perspective.

The Rosie the Riveter Memorial in Marina Bay Park is open year round, dawn to dusk, as are the other Richmond city parks within the National Park's boundaries.

The Rosie Memorial in October 2007.

Rosie Memorial

The park's creation was spurred by the construction of a Rosie the Riveter memorial in a city shoreline park (three years prior to the creation of the National Park), to honor the "Rosies", women who made up much of the workforce at the shipyards. The four Richmond shipyards with their combined 27 shipways, produced 747 ships, more than any other shipyard complex in the country. Richmond was home to 56 different war industries, more than any other city of its size in the United States. The city grew nearly overnight from 24,000 people to 100,000 people, overwhelming the available housing stock, roads, schools, businesses and community services.

The effort behind the memorial was initiated by then-Councilwoman Donna Powers. It grew under Project Director Donna Graves to become the first national tribute to home front American women.

The memorial is located at Marina Bay Park, the site of former Kaiser Richmond Shipyard #2. It is the length of a Liberty ship with a form of the ship being built. The simple metal pier represents the stern at the water's edge, a simple cylinder frame is the smoke stack, and the bow is made of prefabricated parts similar to those assembled by the shipyard workers. A timeline of World War II is placed along the walkway running the length of the memorial. Interpretive panels within the structures present information on women's history, labor history, and the Home Front.

Ford Richmond Plant

Main article: Ford Richmond Plant

The Ford Motor Company Assembly Plant was the largest assembly plant to be built on the West Coast. One of only three tank depots in the entire country, approximately 49,000 jeeps were assembled and 91,000 other military vehicles were processed here. Ford employed thousands of workers at the site during World War II, many of them women who were entering the work force for the first time. "Rosie the Riveter" was a period song representing these women.

In mobilizing the wartime production effort to its full potential, Federal military authorities and private industry began to work closely together on a scale never seen before in American history. This laid the groundwork for what became known as the "military-industrial complex" during the Cold War years.

Noted architect Albert Kahn is credited with the design of the Ford plant in Richmond. After World War II, Ford moved its Northern California factory to Milpitas, where it became known as the San Jose Assembly Plant.

Richmond Shipyards

Main article: Richmond Shipyards

The four Richmond Shipyards were part of the Kaiser Shipyards. The construction of 747 ships during the war here is a feat not equaled anywhere else in the world, before or since. The park's Rosie memorial is located on the former grounds of Shipyard #2. Shipyard #3 is listed on the National Register of Historic Places.

Both Liberty and Victory ships were constructed here. These ships were completed in two-thirds the amount of time and at a quarter of the cost of the average of all other shipyards. The SS *Robert E. Peary* was assembled in less than five days as a part of a special competition among shipyards; but by 1944 it was only taking the astonishingly brief time of a little over two weeks to assemble a Liberty ship by standard methods.

SS *Red Oak Victory*

Main article: SS Red Oak Victory

The SS *Red Oak Victory* is a Victory ship preserved as a museum ship. It was one of 414 Victories built during World War II (constructed at the Richmond Shipyards), but one of only a few of these ships to be transferred from the Merchant Marine to the U.S. Navy. The vessel issued cargo and munitions to various ships in the fleet throughout 1945. During a hazardous tour of duty in the Pacific, SS *Red Oak Victory* handled many tons of ammunition, supplying the fleet without a single casualty.

Atchison Village Housing Project

Main article: Atchison Village, Richmond, California

The huge explosion of workers coming to live in cities like Richmond, caused intense strain on city infrastructure. One of these strains was the severe lack of housing. Workers arriving in these rapidly expanding urban centers were forced to find what they could. They slept in all night movie houses, shared "hot beds" (where three people used one bed, each getting an 8 hour stretch), or just camped out.

Atchison Village Housing Project is an example of the local-Federal collaboration that provided much needed housing and domestic support for defense workers and their families. The modest, wood-frame buildings clearly reflect the constraints (time, money and materials) placed on publicly-funded housing construction during the period. Just prior to and during the war, the Lanham Act of 1940 provided $150 million to the Federal Works Administration, which built approximately 625,000 units of housing in conjunction with local authorities nationwide. These were highly sought after and company managers were the most likely to be able to procure housing in Atchison Village.

Due to racial discrimination, minorities fared very poorly in gaining housing. They often lived in shacks, in the crates that brought the raw materials to the city, in trailers, or in automobiles. They and other lower income earning workers were lucky when they were able to move to barrack-like dormitories constructed for the mass of WWII workers.

The Richmond Housing Authority was selected to be the first authority in the country to manage a defense project. Atchison Village represents one of 20 public housing projects built in Richmond before and during World War II. Constructed in 1941 as Richmond's first public defense housing project, it is the only project funded by the Lanham Act that still exists in Richmond, and one of the few in the nation not destroyed after the war.

Today, Atchison Village is a collection of privately owned houses managed by a cooperative of the homeowners. While most of the dormitories and other low income housing of WWII are gone, Atchison Village, built as permanent housing, remains.

Kaiser Richmond Field Hospital

Main article: Kaiser Richmond Field Hospital

More American workers died in Home Front accidents then US soldiers killed on WWII battlefields. This was true up to the Battle of Normandy in June 1944. Henry J. Kaiser, owner of the Richmond Shipyards, realized that only a healthy work force could meet the deadlines and construction needs of wartime America. He institutionalized a revolutionary idea, pre-paid medical care for workers, which soon expanded beyond workers. For many workers, this was the first time they had seen a doctor.

The Kaiser Richmond Field Hospital for the Richmond Shipyards was financed by the U.S. Maritime Commission, and opened on August 10, 1942.

By August 1944, 92.2 percent of all Richmond shipyard employees had joined the plan, the first voluntary group plan in the country to feature group medical practice, prepayment and substantial medical facilities on such a large scale.By 1990, Kaiser Permanente was still the country's largest nonprofit HMO.

In part due to wartime materials rationing, the Field Hospital is a single-story wood frame structure designed in a simple modernist mode. The Field Hospital operated as a Kaiser Permanente hospital until closing in 1995.

Maritime and Ruth Powers Child Development Centers

The Maritime and Ruth Powers Child Development Centers were two of approximately 35 nursery school units of varying sizes established in the Richmond area during World War II in order to provide child care for women working in the Kaiser shipyards. The Maritime center was funded and constructed by the Maritime Commission as part of a larger development that also included housing, an elementary school and a fire station. The temporary housing was demolished after the war but a larger permanent housing complex remains as do the other buildings.

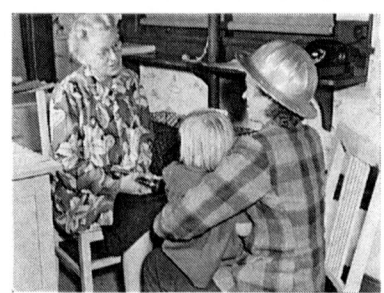

Midnight-shift shipyard worker Arlene Corbin (right) brings her daughter to a day care facility before going home to sleep.

The Maritime Child Development Center, a wood frame, modernist style building operated by the Richmond School District, incorporated progressive educational programming, and was staffed with nutritionists, psychiatrists and certified teachers. It had a capacity of 180 children per day. At its peak, with 24,500 women on the Kaiser payroll, Richmond's citywide child care program maintained a total daily attendance of 1,400 children. Unlike the Federally-funded WPA day care facilities implemented during the New Deal, the World War II centers were not intended for use by the destitute, but for working mothers.

The Kaiser-sponsored Child Care Centers, particularly those at Kaiser's industrial sites in Vanport, Oregon, and Vancouver, Washington, gained a reputation for innovative and high quality child care. The center is still in operation today.

Lucretia Edwards Shoreline Park

Lucretia Edwards Shoreline Park, named in honor of local community activist Lucretia W. Edwards, honors the wartime contributions made by the Bay Area Shipyards during World War II.

In addition to the local Richmond Shipyards, shipworker's bootprints with plaques set in the sidewalks and long low seating walls point visitors to the other Bay Area shipyards.

The following inscriptions are engraved into the concrete walls:

- Bethlehem San Francisco - The only privately owned shipyard in the nation to operate a submarine repair base, this 16th Street yard overhauled 31 subs in two years.
- Moore Dry Dock handled the difficult jobs of production, repair and conversion that slowed overall output in other yards.
- Hunter Point Naval Dry Dock - Hunter Point repaired 600 fighting and support ships.
- Mare Island Naval Shipyard - Mare Island built more than 400 vessels. Mare Island Naval Shipyard set a shipbuilding record for a destroyer that was never broken completing the USS Ward in just 17 1/2 days.

- Marinship - The 75,000 Americans who poured into Marinship during the war years build 93 ships.

See also
- Port Chicago Naval Magazine National Memorial

References
⊚ *This article incorporates public domain material* [1] *from websites or documents of the National Park Service.*

External links
- National Park Service: Rosie the Riveter/World War II Home Front NHP [1]
- Rosie the Riveter Trust, the non-profit partner to Rosie the Riveter/World War II Home Front NHP [2]
- Ford-National Parks Foundation Site [3]

<tr style="height:2px"><td><tr><td colspan=2 style="width:100%;padding:0px;;;" class="navbox-list navbox-odd">

National Forests

National Forests	Angeles · Cleveland · Eldorado · Inyo · Klamath · Lassen · Los Padres · Mendocino · Modoc · Plumas · San Bernardino · Sequoia · Shasta-Trinity · Sierra · Six Rivers · Stanislaus · Tahoe
National Wilderness Preservation System	Agua Tibia · Ansel Adams · Bucks Lake · Caribou · Carson-Iceberg · Castle Crags · Cucamonga · Desolation · Dick Smith · Dinkey Lakes · Emigrant · Golden Trout · Hoover · Inyo Mountains · Ishi · Jennie Lakes · John Muir · Kaiser · Marble Mountain · Mokelumne · Mount Shasta Wilderness · North Fork · San Gabriel · Sanhedrin · San Jacinto · San Rafael · Sespe · Siskuyou · Snow Mountain · South Fork Eel River · South Sierra · South Warner · Thousand Lakes · Trinity Alps · Ventana · Yolla Bolly-Middle Eel · Yuki
Other	Butte Valley National Grassland · Giant Sequoia National Monument · Santa Rosa and San Jacinto Mountains National Monument · Smith River National Recreation Area · Shasta-Trinity National Recreation Area

<tr style="height:2px"><td><tr><td colspan=2 style="width:100%;padding:0px;;;" class="navbox-list navbox-even">

State Forests

Boggs Mountain Demonstration · Ellen Pickett · Jackson Demonstration · Las Posadas · LaTour Demonstration · Mount Zion · Mountain Home Demonstration · Soquel Demonstration

<tr style="height:2px"><td><tr><td colspan=2 style="width:100%;padding:0px;;;" class="navbox-list navbox-odd">

National Wildlife Refuges

Antioch Dunes · Bitter Creek · Blue Ridge · Butte Sink · Castle Rock · Clear Lake · Coachella Valley · Colusa · Delevan · Don Edwards San Francisco Bay · Ellicott Slough · Farallon · Guadalupe-Nipomo Dunes · Hopper Mountain · Humboldt Bay · Kern · Lower Klamath · Marin Islands · Merced · Modoc · Pixley · Sacramento · Sacramento River · Salinas River · San Diego Bay · San Diego · San Joaquin River · San Luis · San Pablo Bay · Seal Beach · Sonny Bono Salton Sea · Stone Lakes · Sutter · Tijuana Slough · Tule Lake

<tr style="height:2px"><td><tr><td colspan=2 style="width:100%;padding:0px;;;" class="navbox-list navbox-even">

State Wildlife Areas

Wildlife AreasEcological ReservesMarine Protected Areas

Antelope Valley · Ash Creek · Bass Hill · Battle Creek · Big Lagoon · Big Sandy · Biscar · Butte Valley · Buttermilk Country · Cache Creek · Camp Cady · Cantara/Ney Springs · Cedar Roughs · Cinder Flats · Collins Eddy · Colusa Bypass · Coon Hollow · Cottonwood Creek · Crescent City Marsh · Crocker Meadows · Daugherty Hill · Decker Island · Doyle · Dutch Flat · Eastlker River · Eel River · Elk Creek Wetlands · Elk River · Fay Slough · Feather River · Fitzhugh Creek · Fremont Weir · Grass Lake · Gray Lodge · Green Creek · Grizzly Island · Hallelujah Junction · Heenan Lake · Hill Slough · Hollenbeck Canyon · Honey Lake · Hope Valley · Horseshoe Ranch · Imperial · Indian Valley · Kelso Peak and Old Dad Mountains · Kinsman Flat · Knoxville · Laguna · Lake Berryessa · Lake Earl · Lake Sonoma · Little Panoche Reservoir · Los Banos · Lower Sherman Island · Mad River Slough · Marble Mountains · Mendota · Merrill's Landing · Miner Slough · Monache Meadows · Morro Bay · Moss Landing · Mouth of Cottonwood Creek · Napa-Sonoma Marshes · North Grasslands · O'Neill Forebay · Oroville · Petaluma Marsh · Pickel Meadow · Pine Creek · Point Edith · Putah Creek · Rector Reservoir · Red Lake · Rhode Island · Sacramento River · San Felipe Valley · San Jacinto · San Luis Obispo · San Luis Reservoir · San Pablo Bay · Santa Rosa · Shasta Valley · Silver Creek · Slinkard/Little Antelope · Smithneck Creek · South Fork · Spenceville · Surprise Valley · Sutter Bypass · Tehama · Truckee River · Upper Butte Basin · Volta · Warner Valley · Waukell Creek · West Hilmar · Westlker River · White Slough · Willow Creek · Yolo Bypass

Albany Mudflats · Alkali Sink · Allensworth · Atascadero Creek Marsh · Bair Island · Baldwin Lake · Batiquitos Lagoon · Blue Sky · Boden Canyon · Boggs Lake · Bolsa Chica · Bonny Doon · Buena Vista

Lagoon · Butler Slough · Butte Creek Canyon · Butte Creek House · Buttonwillow · By Day Creek · Calhoun Cut · Canebrake · Carlsbad Highlands · Carmel Bay · Carrizo Canyon · Carrizo Plains · China Point · Clover Creek · Coachella Valley · Coal Canyon · Corte Madera Marsh · Crestridge · Dairy Mart Ponds · Dales Lake · Del Mar Landing · Elkhorn Slough · Estelle Mountain · Fall River Mills · Fish Slough · Fremont Valley · Goleta Slough · Indian Joe Spring · Kaweah · Kerman · King Clone · Laguna Laurel · Loch Lomond Vernal Pool · Lokern · Magnesia Spring · Marin Islands · Mattole River · McGinty Mountain · Morro Dunes · Morro Rock · Napa River · North Table Mountain · Oasis Spring · Panoche Hills · Peytonia Slough · Pine Hill · Piute Creek · Pleasant Valley · Point Lobos · Rancho Jamul · Redwood Shores · River Springs Lakes · Saline Valley · San Dieguito Lagoon · San Elijo Lagoon · San Felipe Creek · San Joaquin River · Santa Rosa Plateau · Springville · Stone Corral · Sycamore Canyon · Sycuan Peak · Thomes Creek · Tomales Bay · Upper Newport Bay · Watsonville Slough · West Mojave Desert · Woodbridge · Yaudanchi

Abalone Cove · Agua Hedionda Lagoon · Albany Mudflats · Anacapa · Anacapa · Año Nuevo · Asilomar · Atascadero Beach · Bair Island · Batiquitos Lagoon · Big Creek · Big Creek · Big Sycamore Canyon · Bodega · Bolsa Chica · Buena Vista Lagoon · Cambria · Cardiff and San Elijo · Carmel Bay · Carmel Pinnacles · Carrington Point · Catalina Marine Science Center · Corte Madera Marsh · Crystal Cove · Dana Point · Del Mar Landing · Doheny · Doheny · Duxbury Reef · Edward F. Ricketts · Elkhorn Slough · Elkhorn Slough · Encinitas · Estero de Limantour · Fagan Marsh · Farallon Islands · Farnsworth Bank · Fort Ross · Gerstle Cove · Goleta Slough · Greyhound Rock · Gull Island · Harris Point · Heisler Park · Hopkins · Irvine Coast · James V. Fitzgerald · Judith Rock · Julia Pfeiffer Burns · La Jolla · Laguna Beach · Lovers Cove (Catalina Island) · Lovers Point · MacKerricher · Manchester and Arena Rock · Marin Islands · Mia J. Tegner · Moro Cojo Slough · Morro Bay · Morro Bay · Morro Beach · Natural Bridges · Niguel · Pacific Grove Marine Gardens · Painted Cave · Peytonia Slough · Piedras Blancas · Piedras Blancas · Pismo · Pismo-Oceano Beach · Point Buchon · Point Buchon · Point Cabrillo · Point Fermin · Point Lobos · Point Reyes Headlands · Point Sur · Point Sur · Portuguese Ledge · Punta Gorda · Redwood Shores · Refugio · Richardson Rock · Robert E. Badham · Robert W. Crown · Russian Gulch · Russian River · Salt Point · San Diego-Scripps · San Dieguito Lagoon · San Elijo Lagoon · Santa Barbara Island · Scorpion · Skunk Point · Sonoma Coast · Soquel Canyon · South Laguna Beach · South Point · Tomales Bay · Upper Newport Bay · Van Damme · Vandenberg · White Rock (Cambria)

<tr style="height:2px"><td><tr><td colspan=2 style="width:100%;padding:0px;;;" class="navbox-list navbox-odd">

National Landscape Conservation System

National Monuments	California Coastal · Carrizo Plain · Santa Rosa and San Jacinto Mountains
National Conservation Areas	California Desert · King Range
Wilderness Areas	Argus Range · Big Maria Mountains · Bigelow Cholla Garden · Bighorn Mountain · Black Mountain · Bright Star · Bristol Mountains · Cadiz Dunes · Carrizo Gorge · Chemehuevi Mountains · Chimney Peak · Chuckwalla Mountains · Chumash · Cleghorn Lakes · Clipper Mountain · Coso Range · Coyote Mountains · Darwin Falls · Dead Mountains · Dick Smith · El Paso Mountains · Fish Creek Mountains · Funeral Mountains · Golden Valley · Grass Valley · Headwaters Forest Reserve · Hollow Hills · Ibex · Indian Pass · Inyo Mountains · Jacumba · Kelso Dunes · Kiavah · Kingston Range · Little Chuckwalla Mountains · Little Picacho · Machesna Mountain · Matilija · Malpais Mesa · Manly Peak · Mecca Hills · Mesquite · Newberry Mountains · Nopah Range · North Algodones Dunes · North Mesquite Mountains · Old Woman Mountains · Orocopia Mountains · Otay Mountain · Owens Peak · Pahrump Valley · Palen/McCoy · Palo Verde Mountains · Picacho Peak · Piper Mountain · Piute Mountains · Red Buttes · Resting Spring Range · Rice Valley · Riverside Mountains · Rodman Mountains · Sacatar Trail · Saddle Peak Hills · San Gorgonio · Santa Lucia · Santa Rosa · Sawtooth Mountains · Sespe · Sheephole Valley · South Nopah Range · Stateline · Stepladder Mountains · Surprise Canyon · Sylvania Mountains · Trilobite · Turtle Mountains · Whipple Mountains ·

<tr style="height:2px"><td><tr><td colspan=2 style="width:100%;padding:0px;;;" class="navbox-list navbox-even">

National Marine Sanctuaries

Channel Islands · Cordell Bank · Gulf of the Farallones · Monterey Bay

<tr style="height:2px"><td><tr><td colspan=2 style="width:100%;padding:0px;;;" class="navbox-list navbox-odd">

National Estuarine Research Reserves

Elkhorn Slough · San Francisco Bay · Tijuana River

<tr style="height:2px"><td><tr><td colspan=2 style="width:100%;padding:0px;;;" class="navbox-list navbox-even">

University of California Natural Reserve System

Año Nuevo Island · Bodega Marine · Box Springs · Boyd Deep Canyon Desert Research Center · Burns Piñon Ridge · Carpinteria Salt Marsh · Chickering American River · Coal Oil Point · Dawson Los Monos Canyon · Eagle Lake Field Station · Elliott Chaparral · Emerson Oaks · Fort Ord · Hastings · James San Jacinto Mountains · Jenny Pygmy Forest · Jepson Prairie · Kendall-Frost Mission Bay Marsh · Kenneth S. Norris Rancho Marino · Landels-Hill Big Creek · McLaughlin · Motte Rimrock · Quail Ridge · Sagehen Creek Field Station · San Joaquin Freshwater Marsh · Santa Cruz Island · Scripps Coastal · Sedgwick · Stebbins Cold Canyon · Stunt Ranch Santa Monica Mountains · Sweeney Granite Mountains Desert Research Center · Valentine Eastern Sierra · Younger Lagoon

<tr style="height:2px;"><td><tr><td class="navbox-abovebelow" style=";background:#ffc94b;" colspan="2">

Heritage registers: World Heritage Sites · World Network of Biosphere Reserves · National Register of Historic Places · National Historic Landmarks · National Natural Landmarks · California Historical Landmarks · California Points of Historical Interest · California Register of Historical Resources

The Life and Times of Rosie the Riveter

The Life and Time of Rosie the Riveter	
Directed by	Connie Field
Produced by	Connie Field
Starring	Wanita Allen Betty Allie Gladys Belcher Lyn Childs Lola Weixel Margaret Wright
Cinematography	Cathy Zheutlin Bonnie Friedman Robert Handley Emiko Omori
Editing by	Lucy Massie Phenix Connie Field
Distributed by	Clarity Films
Release date(s)	September 27, 1980
Running time	65 min
Language	English

The Life and Times of Rosie the Riveter is a 1981 documentary film by Connie Field about the American women who went to work during World War II to do "men's jobs." In 1996, it was selected for preservation in the United States National Film Registry by the Library of Congress as being "culturally, historically, or aesthetically significant".

The film's title refers to "Rosie the Riveter", the cultural icon that represented women who manned the manufacturing plants which produced munitions and material during World War II.

Connie Field got the idea for the film from a California "Rosie the Riveter Reunion", and, with grants from the National Endowment for the Humanities and other charitable sources, conducted interviews with many hundreds of women who had gone into war work. Out of these she choose five representatives—three black, two white—all marvelously lively, intelligent, attractive and articulate women who recall their experiences with a mixtures of pleasant nostalgia and detached bitterness.

The reminiscences are inter cut with the realities of the period – old news, films, recruiting trailers, March of Time ad pop songs such as "Rosie the Riveter".

External links

- Official Site [1]
- *The Life and Time of Rosie the Riveter* [2] at Allmovie
- *The Life and Times of Rosie the Riveter* [3] at the Internet Movie Database

W.A.S.P.

Women Airforce Service Pilots

The **Women Airforce Service Pilots** (WASP) and its predecessor groups the **Women's Flying Training Detachment** (WFTD) and the **Women's Auxiliary Ferrying Squadron** (WAFS) (from September 10, 1942) were pioneering organizations of civilian female pilots employed to fly military aircraft under the direction of the United States Army Air Forces during World War II. The WFTD and WAFS were combined on August 5, 1943, to create the paramilitary WASP organization. The female pilots of the WASP would end up numbering 1,074, each freeing a male pilot for combat service and duties. The WASP flew over 60 million miles in all, in every type of military aircraft. WASPs were granted veteran status in 1977, and given the Congressional Gold Medal in 2009.

Elizabeth L. Gardner, WASP, at the controls of a B-26 Marauder

Twenty-five thousand women applied to join the WASP, but only 1,830 were accepted and took the oath, and out of those only 1,074 women passed the training and joined.

Creation of the WASP

By the summer of 1941, the famous women pilots Jacqueline "Jackie" Cochran and test-pilot Nancy Harkness Love independently submitted proposals for the use of female pilots in non-combat missions to the US Army Air Forces (USAAF, the predecessor to the United States Air Force or USAF) after the outbreak of World War II in Europe. The motivation was to free male pilots for combat roles by employing qualified female pilots on missions such as ferrying aircraft from factories to military bases, and towing drones and aerial targets. Leading into Pearl Harbor, General Henry H. "Hap" Arnold, commander of the USAAF, had turned down both Love's 1940 proposal and the proposal of the better connected and more famous Cochran despite unsubtle lobbying by Eleanor Roosevelt, but essentially promised command of any such effort to Cochran, should such a force be needed in the future.

While the U.S. was not yet fighting in the war, Cochran had gone to England to volunteer to fly for the Air Transport Auxiliary (ATA). The ATA had been using female pilots since January 1940 and was starting to train new ones as well. The American women who flew in the ATA were the first American women to fly military aircraft. They flew the Royal Air Force's front-line aircraft—Spitfires, Typhoons, Hudsons, Mitchells, Blenheims, Oxfords, Walruses, and Sea Otters—in a non-combat role, but in combat-like conditions. Most of these women served the war in the ATA. In fact, only three members of the ATA returned to the U.S. to participate in the WASP program.

Shirley Slade, WASP trainee—*Life* magazine feature story

The U.S. was building its air power and military presence in anticipation of direct involvement in the conflict and had belatedly begun to drastically expand its men in uniform. This period had led to a dramatic increase in activity for the U.S. Army Air Forces, and there were obvious gaps in "manpower" that could be filled by women. However, it was not until after the attack on Pearl Harbor brought U.S. armed forces into the war that it became evident there were not enough male pilots.

To those most involved within the USAAF, especially in the new Ferrying Division of the Air Transport Command (ATC), the numbers were painfully obvious. Ferrying Division commander Brig. Gen. William H. Tunner, in charge of acquiring civilan ferry pilots, decided to integrate a civilian force of female pilots into the AAF after speaking with a fellow ATC staff officer, Major Robert M. Love and his wife Nancy. Convinced of the feasibility of the program by Mrs. Love, who had a Commercial Pilot Licence, he asked her to draw up a proposal, unaware that Arnold had shelved a similar proposal by Tunner's superior, Maj. Gen. Robert Olds.

Cochran had committed to go to Great Britain in March 1942 for a trial program of female pilots with the ATA, and used her association with President and Mrs. Roosevelt to lobby Arnold to reject any plan that did not commission women and set up an independent organization commanded by women. Ironically, Tunner's proposal called for commissioning women in the WAACs, which was turned down after review by Arnold.

By mid-summer of 1942, Arnold was willing to consider the prior proposals seriously. Tunner and Love's plan was reviewed by ATC headquarters, and forwarded by now-commander Gen. Harold L. George to Arnold, who was fully aware of it and gave it his blessing after Mrs. Roosevelt suggested a similar idea in a newspaper column. The Women's Auxiliary Ferry Squadron (WAFS), headed by Mrs.

Love, went into operation on September 10, 1942. Soon the Air Transport Command began using women to ferry planes from factory to air fields.

Cochran returned to the United States on September 10 as the new organization was being publicized, and immediately confronted Arnold for an explanation. Arnold claimed ignorance and blamed the ATC staff, in particular George's chief of staff, Col. (and former president of American Airlines) C. R. Smith. With the publicity involved, the WAFS program could not be reversed, and so on September 15 Cochran's training proposal was also adopted. Cochran and Love's squadrons were thereby established separately: as the 319th Women's Flying Training Detachment (WFTD) at Municipal Airport (now Hobby Airport) in Houston, Texas, with Cochran as commanding officer, and the Women's Auxiliary Ferrying Squadron, 2nd Ferrying Group, at New Castle (Delaware) Army Air Base (now New Castle Airport).

Though rivals, the two programs and their respective leaders operated independently and without acknowledgment of each other until the summer of 1943, when Cochran pushed aggressively for a single entity to control the activity of all women pilots. Although Tunner in particular objected on the basis of differing qualification standards and the absolute necessity of ATC being able to control its own pilots, Cochran's pre-eminence with Arnold prevailed, and in July 1943 he ordered the programs merged, with Cochran as director. The WAFS and the WFTD combined to form the Women Airforce Service Pilots (WASP).

Initial WASP training

WASP training spanned 19 groups of women including The Originals, or WAFS lead by Nancy Love, and The Guinea Pigs—Jacqueline Cochran's first of 18 classes of women pilots. WASPs were required to complete the same primary, basic, and advanced training courses as male Army Air Corps pilots, and many went on to specialized flight training . There were two Chinese-American women in the WASP, Hazel Ying Lee and Maggie Gee (pilot). Ola Mildred Rexroat, an Oglala Sioux woman from Pine Ridge Indian Reservation, South Dakota, was the only Native American woman in the WASP; she survived the war and later joined the Air Force. All the other members of the WASP were white; no African-Americans were allowed to join the WASP.

The WAFS, each with an average of about 1,400 flying hours and a commercial pilot rating, received 30 days of orientation to learn Army paperwork and to fly by military regulations. Afterward, they were assigned to various ferrying commands.

The Guinea Pigs started training at Houston Municipal Airport on November 16, 1942, as part of the 319th Army Air Force Women's Flying Training Detachment (AAFWFTD). This was just after the WAFS had started their orientation in Wilmington, Delaware. Unlike the WAFS, the women that reported to Houston did not have uniforms and had to find their own lodging. The "Woofteddies" (WFTD) also had minimal medical care, no life insurance, no crash truck, no fire truck, a loaned ambulance from Ellington, insufficient administrative staff, and a hodgepodge of aircraft—23 types—for training. As late as January 1943, when the third class was about to start their training, the three classes were described by Byrd Granger in On Final Approach as, "a raggle-taggle crowd in a rainbow of rumpled clothing" as they gathered for morning and evening colors.

This lack of resources was combined with the foggy and wet Houston weather, which delayed the graduation of the first class from February to April. Conditions included the wet sticky clay soil everywhere, and a scarcity of rest rooms; the potential for morale problems was significant. To minimize this, the *Fifinella Gazette* was started. The first issue was published February 10, 1943. The female gremlin Fifinella, conceived by Roald Dahl and drawn by Walt Disney, was used as the official WASP mascot and appeared on their shoulder patches.

The first Houston class started with 38 women with a minimum of 200 hours. Twenty-three graduated on April 24, 1943, at the only Houston WASP graduation at Ellington Army Air Field. The second Houston class, starting in December 1942 with a minimum of 100 hours, finished their training just in time to move to Sweetwater and become the first graduating class from Avenger Field on May 28, 1943. The third class completed their advanced training at Avenger Field and graduated July 3, 1943. Half the fourth class, 76 women, started their primary training in Houston on February 15, 1943, and then transferred to Sweetwater.

On March 7, 1943, the Houston classes incurred their first fatality. Margaret Oldenburg of 43-W-4 and her instructor, Norris G. Morgan, crashed seven miles south of Houston and were killed on impact.

By the end of May 1943, the Houston 319th AAFWFTD was history. Later, in the summer of 1943, both the WAFS and WFTD were renamed WASP.

Duties of the WASP

The WASP women pilots each already had a pilot's license. They were trained to fly "the Army way" by the U.S. Army Air Forces at Avenger Field in Sweetwater, Texas. More than 25,000 women applied for WASP service, and fewer than 1,900 were accepted. After completing four months of military flight training, 1,078 of them earned their wings and became the first women to fly American military aircraft. Except for the fact that the women were not training for combat, their course of instruction was essentially the same as that for aviation cadets. The WASPs thus received no gunnery training and very little formation flying and acrobatics, but went through the maneuvers necessary to be able to recover from any position. The percentage of trainees who were eliminated during training compared favorably with the elimination rates for male cadets in the Central Flying Training Command.

After training, the WASPs were stationed at 120 air bases across the U.S. assuming numerous flight-related missions, relieving male pilots for combat duty. They flew sixty million miles of operational flights from aircraft factories to ports of embarkation and military training bases, towing targets for live anti-aircraft artillery practice and simulated strafing missions, and transporting cargo. Almost every type of aircraft flown by the USAAF during World War II was also flown at some point by women in these roles. In addition, a few exceptionally qualified women were allowed to test rocket-propelled planes, to pilot jet-propelled planes, and to work with radar-controlled targets. Between September 1942 and December 1944, the WASP delivered 12,650 aircraft of 78 different types. Over fifty percent of the ferrying of combat aircraft within the United States during the war was carried out by WASP pilots.

Thirty-eight WASP fliers lost their lives while serving during the war — 11 in training and 27 on active duty, all in accidents. Because they were not considered to be in the military under the existing guidelines, a fallen WASP was sent home at family expense without traditional military honors or note of heroism. The army would not even allow the U.S. flag to be put on fallen WASP pilots' coffins.

Battle for militarization

The WASP were civil service employees and did not receive military benefits, unlike their male counterparts. On the other hand, they were not administratively tied to the Army Air Forces and could resign at any time after completion of their training, although few if any did.[citation needed]

Frances Green, Margaret (Peg) Kirchner, Ann Waldner and Blanche Osborn leaving their plane, "Pistol Packin' Mama," at the four-engine school at Lockbourne AAF, Ohio, during WASP ferry training B-17 Flying Fortress

On 30 September 1943 the first of the WASP militarization bills was introduced in the United States House of Representatives. Both Cochran and Arnold desired a separate corps headed by a woman colonel (similar to the WAC, WAVES, SPAR, and Marine heads). The War Department, however, consistently opposed such a move, since there was no separate corps for male pilots as distinguished from nonrated AAF officers. Instead, it preferred that women be commissioned in the WAC and thus added to some 2,000 "Air WAC" officers already assigned, for whom flying duty was then legally permissible.[citation needed]

On June 21, 1944, the bill in the House to give the WASP military status was narrowly defeated after civilian male pilots, reacting to closure of some civilian flight training schools and termination of two male pilot training commissioning programs, lobbied against the bill. The House Committee on the Civil Service (Ramspeck Committee) reported on June 5, 1944, that it considered the WASP was unnecessary, and unjustifiably expensive, and recommended that the recruiting and training of inexperienced women pilots be halted.[citation needed]

Cochran had been pushing for a resolution of the question, in effect delivering an ultimatum to either commission the women or disband the program. The AAF had developed an excess of pilots and pilot candidates, and as a result, Arnold (who had been a proponent of militarization) ordered that the WASP be disbanded by December 20, 1944. Arnold is quoted from a speech he delivered at Avenger Field in

Sweetwater, Texas on December 7, 1944:

> The WASP have completed their mission. Their job has been successful. But as is usual in war, the cost has been heavy. Thirty-eight WASP have died while helping their country move toward the moment of final victory. The Air Forces will long remember their service and their final sacrifice.

At the conclusion of the WASP program there were 916 women pilots on duty with the AAF, with 620 assigned to the Training Command, 141 to the Air Transport Command, 133 to the numbered air forces in the Continental United States, 11 to the Weather Wing, 9 to the technical commands, and one to the Troop Carrier Command.[citation needed]

Legacy

All records of the WASP were classified and sealed for 35 years, so their contributions to the war effort were little known and inaccessible to historians. In 1975, under the leadership of Col. Bruce Arnold, son of General Hap Arnold, the WASPs fought the "Battle of Congress" in Washington, D.C., to belatedly obtain recognition as veterans of World War II. They organized as a group again and tried to gain public support for their official recognition. Finally, in 1977, the records were unsealed after an Air Force press release erroneously stated the Air Force was training the first women to fly military aircraft for the U.S.

Madge Moore showing the Daedalian Fighter Flight (Nellis AFB, NV) the WASP Congressional Gold Medal she was presented in Washington, D.C.

This time, the WASPs lobbied Congress with the important support of Senator Barry Goldwater, who himself had been a World War II ferry pilot in the 27th Ferry Squadron. President Jimmy Carter signed legislation #95-202, Section 401, The G.I. Bill Improvement Act of 1977, granting the WASP corps full military status for their service. In 1984, each WASP was awarded the World War II Victory Medal. Those who served for more than one year were also awarded American Theater Ribbon/American Campaign Medal for their service during the war. Many of the medals were accepted by the recipients' sons and daughters on their behalf.[citation needed]

Because of the pioneering and the expertise they demonstrated in successfully flying military aircraft, the WASP pilots' record showed that women pilots, when given the same training as men pilots, were as capable as men in non-combat flying.[citation needed]

In July 2009, President Barack Obama signed the WASP Congressional Gold Medal into law.

On July 1, 2009 President Barack Obama and the United States Congress awarded the WASP the Congressional Gold Medal. Three of the roughly 300 surviving WASPs were on hand to witness the event. During the ceremony President Obama said, "The Women Airforce Service Pilots courageously answered their country's call in a time of need while blazing a trail for the brave women who have given and continue to give so much in service to this nation since. Every American should be grateful for their service, and I am honored to sign this bill to finally give them some of the hard-earned recognition they deserve." On March 10, 2010, 200 surviving WASPs came to the US Capitol to accept the Congressional Gold Medal from House Speaker Nancy Pelosi and other Congressional leaders.

Notable WASP aviators

- Mildred Darlene "Micky" Tuttle Axton — A licensed pilot since 1940 (the only woman in her flight class at Coffeyville, Kan., Junior College), she was a member of WASP 43-W-7, but left the organization in April 1944 when her mother became ill. Micky at that time applied for a job with Boeing and was hired as a flight test engineer, in May 1944 becoming the first woman ever to fly the B-29 Superfortress. The Jayhawk Wing of the Commemorative Air Force operates a restored Fairchild PT-19 dubbed "Miss Micky" in her honor. Micky's brother, Ralph Tuttle, was an Army Air Corps fighter pilot in the Pacific Theater of Operations, earning the Silver Star and twice being awarded the Distinguished Flying Cross.

Jackie Cochran (center) with WASP trainees

- Ann Baumgartner Carl
- Jacqueline Cochran — Director of the WASP. In 1938, Cochran became famous nationwide for winning the Bendix Transcontinental Race.
- Rosa Charlyne Creger
- Nancy Batson Crews
- Cornelia Fort — One of the original WAFS. Fort's experience included evading Japanese attacking planes at Pearl Harbor on December 7, 1941.
- Maggie Gee one of only two Asian-Americans in the WASP, the other being Hazel Ying Lee
- Betty Gillies

- Lois Hailey
- Sara Payne Hayden
- Celia Hunter
- Marge Hurlburt — Held the woman's international airspeed record before her death in 1947.
- Teresa James
- Shirley C. Kruse
- Hazel Ying Lee, one of two Asian-Americans in the WASP, the other being Maggie Gee.
- Barbara Erickson London — Was the only WASP member to be awarded the Air Medal during World War II. Following the war, medals were awarded to other WASP members.
- Nancy Love
- Annabelle Craft Moss
- Anne Noggle — Following the war she became a noted photographer and writer.
- Suzanne Upjohn DeLano Parish, co-founder of Kalamazoo Air Museum.
- Deanie Bishop Parrish
- Mabel Rawlinson
- Ola Mildred Rexroat, an Oglala Sioux from Pine Ridge Indian Reservation, South Dakota, was the only Native American woman in the WASP [1].
- Margaret Ringenberg
- Gloria Heath
- Dawn Rochow Seymour
- Evelyn Sharp—In 1938, Evelyn Sharp was the youngest person in the United States to receive a commercial pilots license.
- Gertrude Tompkins Silver — the last WASP to go missing in World War II. She made a flight from Mines Field (currently LAX) to Palm Springs on October 26, 1944, intending to fly a P-51 Mustang on to New Jersey, but never arrived in Palm Springs. As of Jan. 2010, search efforts to locate the crash site are still ongoing.
- Dora Dougherty Strother
- Ginny Hill Wood
- Carla Horowitz

Fictional depiction

- Season 1, Episode 22 of Baa Baa Black Sheep was entitled W*A*S*P*S. It first aired on 1 March 1977. The episode was factually inaccurate, the WASP never flew overseas, and there is no "s" at the end of the name, since the name itself is plural.
- In 1984, Janet Dailey published *Silver Wings, Santiago Blue,* a fictional novel of the WASP. (Santiago Blue was the official name for the blue color of the WASP uniforms).
- In the modern *Wonder Woman* continuity, Steve Trevor's mother, Diana Trevor, was a WASP who inadvertently crashlanded on Themyscira on a mission in the 1940s and died helping the Amazons fight an attacking menace.
- The 2008 TV movie *Warbirds* features a WASP B-29 crew whose plane is commandeered for a secret mission but crashes on a pteranodon-infested island.
- A 2009 episode of the TV show *Cold Case* features the investigators looking for the murderer of a WASP after her plane is found in modern day Philadelphia, Pennsylvania.
- Sherri L. Smith's 2009 teen book *Flygirl* is about an 18-year-old African American woman who passes as white so she can serve in the WASP.
- A 2009 episode of *Army Wives* featured a flashback to WWII. One of the wives was a WASP.

See also

- Women Airforce Service Pilots Badge
- Women's Auxiliary Air Force (WAAF – British)
- Air Transport Auxiliary – UK included many civilian female pilots
- Women's Auxiliary Australian Air Force (WAAAF)
- Royal Canadian Air Force Women's Division (RCAFWD)
- Women's Army Corps (WAC)
- WAVES – Women Accepted for Volunteer Emergency Service
- SPARS – United States Coast Guard Women's Reserve
- Women in the Air Force (WAF)
- United States Army Air Forces
- United States Air Force
- Avenger Field Airport

Further reading

- Granger, Byrd Howell. *On Final Approach: The Women Airforce Service Pilots of W.W.II*. Falconer Publishing Co., 1991.
- Haynsworth, Leslie, and David Toomey. *Amelia Earhart's Daughters*. William Morrow and Company, 1998.
- Keil, Sally VanWagenen, *Those Wonderful Women in Their Flying Machines: The Unknown Heroines of World War II*. New York: Four Directions Press, 1990. ISBN 0-9627659-0-2.
- Merryman, Molly. *Clipped Wings: The Rise and Fall of the Women Airforce Service Pilots (WASPs) of World War II*. New York: New York University Press, 1998. ISBN 0814755682.
- Noggle, Anne. *For God, Country and the Thrill of It: Women Airforce Service Pilots During WWII*. Texas A&M Unoversity Press. 1990
- Regis, Margaret. *When Our Mothers Went to War: An Illustrated History of Women in World War II*. [1] Seattle: NavPublishing, 2008. ISBN 978-1-87732-05-0.
- Rickman, Sarah Byrn. *Nancy Batson Crews: Alabama's First Lady of Flight*. University of Alabama Press. 2009
- Schrader, Helena. *Sisters in Arms: British and American Women Pilots During World War II*. Pen and Sword Books, 2006.
- Simbeck, Rob. *Daughter of the Air: The Brief Soaring Life of Corne;ia Fort*. Atlantic Monthly Press. 1999.
- Strebe, Amy Goodpaster. *Flying for her Country: The American and Soviet Women Military Pilots of World War II*. Potomac Books. 2009
- Williams, Vera S. *WASPs: Women Airforce Service Pilots of World War II*. Osceola, Minnesota: Motorbooks International, 1994. ISBN 0-87938-856-0.

Helen W. Snapp, WASP, Washington, D.C., Low-target Squadron, Camp Stewart, Georgia, June 1944

External links

- WASP Awarded Congressional Gold Medal [2], March 10, 2010
- The National WASP World War II Museum [3]
- Texas Woman's University: Women Airforce Service Pilots Collection [4] TWU maintains the official WASP archives and includes oral histories, photographs, and other archival collections on the WASP.

- Wings Across America [5]; a digital video history project, seeking to document the WASPs of World War II.
- WASP on the WEB [6] 2,000 pages of WASP information, photos, videos
- Women Airforce Service Pilots (WASP) Remembered by those who knew them [7]
- Nancy Love and the WASP Ferry Pilots of World War II [8]
- Women in the U.S. Army [9]
- PBS American Experience: Fly Girls [10] Website for the PBS documentary on the WASP.
- Blitzkrieg Baby [6]—Information on World War II U.S. women's service organizations, including uniforms.
- USAF Museum: Women Pilots in World War II History [11]—Air Force Museum virtual exhibit.
- Winged Auxiliaries: Women Pilots in the UK and US during World War Two [12]—Draws comparisons between British ATA and American WASP pilots in World War II.
- Dwight D. Eisenhower Presidential Library's archives [13]—information and documentation about the WASPs and Jacqueline Cochran.
- Thirty-eight women earned their second pair of wings during the WASP program [14]
- The account of the discovery of the site of a B-25 crash which killed a WASP pilot; some of her effects were found. [15]

National Museum of the USAF fact sheets

- Air Transport Auxiliary [16]
- WASPS: Breaking Ground for Today's Female USAF Pilots [17]
- Women's Auxiliary Ferry Squadron [18]
- Nancy Harkness Love Biography [19]
- Description of Fifinella from USAF website [20]
- WASPS Demonstrate their Abilities [21]
- WASP Disbanded [22]
- WASP Epilogue [23]
- Women Pilots with the AAF, 1941–1944 [24]

The U.S.O.

United Service Organizations

Type	Services
Founded	4 February 1941
Location	Arlington, VA
Key people	Sloan D. Gibson President and CEO
Area served	160 centers worldwide
Focus	morale, welfare and recreational services to U.S. military personnel and their families
Revenue	Contributions
Volunteers	44,000
Motto	*Until Every One Comes Home*
Website	USO Home [1]

The **United Service Organizations Inc.** (**USO**) is a private, nonprofit organization that provides morale and recreational services to members of the U.S. military, with programs in 140 centers worldwide. Since 1941, it has worked in partnership with the Department of Defense (DOD), and has provided support and entertainment to U.S. armed forces, relying heavily on private contributions and on funds, goods, and services from DOD. Although congressionally chartered, it is not a government agency.

During World War II, the USO became the G.I.'s "home away from home" and began a tradition of entertaining the troops that continues today. Involvement in the USO was one of the many ways in which the nation had come together to support the war effort, with nearly 1.5 million Americans having volunteered their services in some way. After it was disbanded in 1947, it was revived in 1950 for the Korean War, after which it also provided peacetime services. During the Vietnam War, USOs were sometimes located in combat zones.

The organization became particularly famous for its live performances called *Camp Shows*, through which the entertainment industry helped boost the morale of its servicemen and women. Hollywood in general was eager to show its patriotism, and lots of big names joined the ranks of USO entertainers. They entertained in military bases both at home and overseas, often placing their own lives in danger by traveling or performing under hazardous conditions.

Today the USO has over 160 locations around the world in 11 countries (including the U.S.) and 23 states. In 2009, USO centers served 7.7 million visitors. In 2008, Sloan Gibson became the 22nd President and CEO. Brigadier General (Retired) John I. Pray, Jr., joined the USO in 2009 as Senior Vice President of Entertainment and Programs. In 2010, Rear Admiral Frank Thorp IV (USN, ret.) joined the organization as the Senior Vice President of Marketing and Communications.

History

Mission and goals

The USO was founded in 1941 in response to a request from President Franklin D. Roosevelt to provide morale and recreation services to U.S. uniformed military personnel. Roosevelt was elected as its honorary chairman. This request brought together six civilian organizations: the Salvation Army, Young Men's Christian Association (YMCA), Young Women's Christian Association (YWCA), National Catholic Community Service, National Travelers Aid Association and the National Jewish Welfare Board. They were brought together under one umbrella to support U.S. troops. Roosevelt said he wanted "these private organizations to handle the on-leave recreation of the men in the armed forces." According to historian Emily Yellin, "The government was to build the buildings and the USO was to raise private funds to carry out its main mission: boosting the morale of the military."

The first national campaign chairman was Thomas Dewey, who raised $16 million in the first year. The second chairman was Prescott Bush, a future senator and father to one future president, and the grandfather to another. The USO was incorporated in New York February 4, with the first facility erected in DeRidder, Louisiana,1941. More USO centers and clubs opened around the world as a "Home Away from Home" for GIs. The USO club was a place to go for dances and social events, for movies and music, for a quiet place to talk or write a letter home, or for a free cup of coffee and an egg.

The USO also brought Hollywood celebrities and volunteer entertainers to perform for the troops. According to movie historian Steven Cohan, "most of all ... in taking home on the road, it equated the nation with showbiz. USO camp shows were designed in their export to remind soldiers of home." They did this, he noted, by "nurturing in troops a sense of patriotic identification with America through popular entertainment." An article in *Look* magazine at the time, stated, "For the little time the show lasts, the men are taken straight to the familiar Main Street that is the goal of every fighting American far away from home." Maxene Andrews wrote, "The entertainment brought home to the boys. *Their* home." Actor George Raft stated at the beginning of the war, "Now it's going to be up to us to send to the men here and abroad real, living entertainment, the songs, the dances, and the laughs they had back home."

USO promotional literature stated its goals:

"The story of USO camp shows belongs to the American people, for it was their contribution that made it possible. It is an important part in the life of your sons, your brothers, your husbands, and your sweethearts."

World War II

After being formed in 1941 in response to World War II, "centers were established quickly... in churches, barns, railroad cars, museums, castles, beach clubs, and log cabins." Most centers offered recreational activities, such as holding dances and showing movies. And there were the well-known free coffee and doughnuts. Some USO bases provided a haven for spending a quiet moment alone or writing a letter home, while others offered spiritual guidance and made childcare available for military wives.

Bob Hope USO show, 1944

But the organization became mostly known for its live performances called *Camp Shows*, through which the entertainment industry helped boost the morale of its servicemen and women. At its high point in 1944, the USO had more than 3,000 clubs, and curtains were rising on USO shows 700 times a day. From 1941 to 1947, the USO presented more than 400,000 performances, featuring entertainers such as Bing Crosby, Judy Garland, Bette Davis, Humphrey Bogart, Lauren Bacall, Frank Sinatra, Marlene Dietrich, Hattie McDaniel, Eubie Blake, Ann Sheridan, Laurel and Hardy, The Marx Brothers, Jack Benny, Larry Adler, Zero Mostel, James Cagney, James Stewart, Gary Cooper, Doraine and Ellis, Lena Horne, Danny Kaye, The Rockettes, Al Jolson, Fred Astaire, Curly Joe DeRita, The Andrews Sisters, Joe E. Brown, Joe E. Lewis, Ray Bolger, Lucille Ball, Glenn Miller, Martha Raye, Mickey Rooney, Betty Hutton, Dinah Shore, and most famously, Bob Hope.

The USO's fundraising efforts were not without controversy. An MGM film, *Mr. Gardenia Jones*, created to assist the USO in its fundraising campaign, was nearly withdrawn from theaters due to objections by the War Department. The objections were centered around scenes showing soldiers jumping with joy at the opportunity to shower in canteens and rest in overstuffed and comfortable USO chairs. The Army, noted the *New York Times*, "feels this is not good for morale as it implies that there are no showers or other comforts for soldiers in military camps." The film starred Ronald Reagan, who was then a captain in the Army.

Fundraising was also aided by private entertainment groups. Songwriter Irving Berlin took the entire 100-person, all-soldier cast of his Broadway production "This Is the Army," on tour in Europe in 1942, raising nearly $10 million for the Army Emergency Relief Fund. The following year the show was made into a film by the same title, again starring Ronald Reagan. One of the highlights of the film was its introduction of Berlin's song, "God Bless America," considered one of the nation's most patriotic songs.

War correspondent Quentin Reynolds, in an article for *Billboard magazine* in 1943, wrote, "Entertainment, all phases of it -- radio, pictures and live -- should be treated as essential. You don't know what entertainment means to the guys who do the fighting until you've been up there with the men yourself. . . . You can quote me as saying that we should use entertainment as an essential industry so long as it's for the boys in service. Anybody who has been there would insist on it. . . . Hell, you should have seen how happy the G.I.'s were when they heard the ballplayers were coming over. And John Steinbeck, just back from a chore as war correspondent, . . . also applauded show business as part of the war effort and its importance as a morale builder."

Looking back after the war

According to historian Paul Holsinger, between 1941 and 1945, the USO did 293,738 performances in 208,178 separate visits. Estimates were that more than 161 million servicemen and women, in the U.S. and abroad, were entertained. The USO also did shows in military hospitals, eventually entertaining more than 3 million wounded soldiers and sailors in 192 different hospitals. There were 702 different USO troupes that toured the world, some spending up to six months per tour. In 1943, a United States Liberty ship named the SS *U.S.O.* was launched. She was scrapped in 1967.

Irving Berlin singing aboard USS Arkansas, 1944

Twenty-eight performers died in the course of their tours, from plane crashes, illness, or diseases contracted while on tour. In one such instance in 1943, a plane carrying a U.S.O. troupe crashed outside

Lisbon, killing singer and actress Tamara Drasin, and severely injuring Broadway singer Jane Froman. Froman returned to Europe on crutches in 1945 to again entertain the troops. She later married the co-pilot who saved her life in that crash, and her true story was made into the 1952 film *With a Song in My Heart*, with Froman providing the actual singing voice. Others, such as Al Jolson, the first entertainer to go overseas in World War II, contracted malaria, resulting in the loss of his lung, cutting short his tour.

In 1942, about seven months after the war began, CBS went on the air with a weekly radio variety show called *Stagedoor Canteen*. The show remained on the air for the duration of the war and became one of the nation's most popular. In 1943, United Artists released a reality-style movie about the USO called *Stage Door Canteen*, and the following year Warner Brothers produced a similar movie, called *Hollywood Canteen*. In 1991, 20th Century Fox produced the film, *For the Boys*, which told the story of two USO performers, and starred Bette Midler and James Caan. It covered a 50-year timespan, from the USO's inception in 1941 through Operation Desert Storm, in 1991. Another movie was planned in 1950 but never made. Just 10 days after Al Jolson returned from entertaining troops in Korea, he agreed with RKO producers to star in a new movie, *Stars and Stripes for Ever,* about a U.S.O. troupe in the South Pacific during World War II. Unfortunately, he died a week later as a result of physical exhaustion from his tour.

By the war's end, Steven Cohan concludes that "the USO amounted to the biggest enterprise American show business has ever tackled. The audience was millions of American fighting men, the theatre's location: the world, the producer: USO camp shows"

Women in the USO

According to Emily Yellin, many of the key foot soldiers in the USO's mission were women who were "charged with providing friendly diversion for U.S. troops who were mostly men in their teens and twenties." USO centers throughout the world recruited female volunteers to serve doughnuts, dance, and just talk with the troops. USO historian Julia Carson writes that this "nostalgic hour," designed to cheer and comfort soldiers, involved "listening to music - American style" and "looking at pretty girls, like no other pretty girls in the world - American girls."

African American women "scrambled to rally the community around the soldiers and create programs for them." By 1946, hostesses had served more than two thousand soldiers a day while also providing facilities for the wounded and convalescent who were on leave. They went to black businesses and fraternal organizations in order to find sponsorship for their USO group, and later expanded to fulfill the needs of soldiers during the Korean war. Moreover, they worked to merge black and white USOs into one desegregated unit. As black historian Megan Shockley noted, "Their work for the desegregation of USOs had begun during World War II, and it finally paid off."

Women were also key entertainers who performed at shows. Stars such as Marlene Dietrich, Judy Garland, Betty Grable and Rita Hayworth had traveled over a million miles. Yellin notes that on one tour, Hayworth visited six camps, gave thousands of autographs, and "came back from Texas with a full-fledged nervous breakdown from over-enthusiasm!" Opera singer Lily Pons, after she had performed a "serious" opera song to troops in Burma, "an applause erupted that stunned even the most seasoned performers." She later wrote in a letter, "Every woman back home wears a halo now, and those who represent her had better keep theirs on, too."

Author Joeie Dee pointed out that "for women entertainers, traveling with the USO made it possible to be patriots and adventurers as well as professionals." She adds, however, that the G.I.s in the USO audiences "tended to see these women in a different light - as reminders of and even substitutes for their girls back home, as a reward for fighting the war, as embodiments of what they were fighting for." Edward Skvarna, now 84, remembers 1943, when he met Donna Reed at a U.S.O. canteen and asked her to dance. "I had never danced with a celebrity before, so I felt delighted, privileged even, to meet her. . . . But I really felt she was like a girl from back home." Jay Fultz, author of her biography, states that soldiers "often wrote to her as if to a sister or the girl next door, confiding moments of homesickness, loneliness, privation and anxiety."

Women entertainers

One female entertainer wrote about conditions while performing:

> "We've played to audiences, many of them ankle deep in mud, huddled under the ponchos in the pouring rain (it breaks your heart the first two or three times to see men so hungry for entertainment.) We've played on uncovered stages, when we, as well as the audience, got rain-soaked. We've played with huge tropical bugs flying in our hair and faces; we've played to audiences of thousands of men, audiences spreading from our very feet to far up a hillside and many sitting in the trees. . . . We've played to audiences in small units of 500 or so, and much oftener to audiences of 8 to 10,000. Every night we play a different place."

Singer and dancer Ann Miller described performing for badly wounded soldiers. She did forty-eight shows for "broken soldiers," who were mostly lying on stretchers in the lobbies of hotels, watching as she entertained them. Yellin writes, "During her last show she collapsed and had to be taken home on an Army airplane." Afterwards, Miller described the experience:

US Coast Guard, 1st show in Vietnam, 1970

> "We went from ward to ward to ward, singing and dancing and trying to boost the morale of these men. It was just hell. . . . I just fell apart and I think the shock of seeing those men with their arms and legs blown off - it was just frightening. But when you do it, you do it. You try to help them, try to sing and dance. You try to keep their spirits up. It's heartbreaking."

Korean War

In the 1940s the USO was disbanded due partly to lack of funds. However, in 1950, when the United States entered the Korean War, Secretary of Defense George Marshall and Secretary of the Navy Francis Matthews requested that the USO be reactivated "to provide support for the men and women of the armed forces with help of the American people" According to war historian Paul Edwards, Between 1952 and 1953, not a day went by without the USO providing services somewhere in Korea. At home or overseas, in 1952 it was serving 3.5 million in the armed forces using much the same methods of operation as it did in World War II.

Many stars, both well-known and new, came to perform, including Bob Hope, Errol Flynn, Debbie Reynolds, Donald O'Connor, Piper Laurie, Jane Russell, Paul Douglas, Terry Moore, Marilyn Monroe, Danny Kaye, Rory Calhoun, Mickey Rooney, Jayne Mansfield, Al Jolson and many others. Jolson notably was the first to volunteer and traveled to Korea at his own expense (he was also the first to entertain troops during World War II.)

Veterans have recalled many of the USOs events, sometimes in vivid detail:

> "On that cold, overcast day, there were more than five thousand troops in the audience. They sat on the ground or up on the hillside. When everyone was settled, Danny Kaye opened the show by going to the microphone, looking at his large audience, and shouting, "Who's holding back the enemy?" The GIs roared with laughter. We were thrilled to have Kaye and his entertainers in our

area. We especially liked the young women in the show. Danny was okay, with his stories and jokes, but after all, we knew what American men looked like."[:51]

Author Linda Granfield in describing the show, writes, "For two hours, the men could forget they were soldiers at war. After the show, they returned to the fighting in the hills. Some in that audience never made it back." By the end of the war, over 113,000 American USO volunteers were working at 294 centers at home and abroad." And 126 units had given 5,422 performances to servicemen in Korea and the wounded in Japan

Vietnam War

The USO was in Vietnam before the first combat troops arrived, with the first USO club opened in Saigon in April, 1963. The 23 centers in Vietnam and Thailand served as many as a million service members a month, and the USO presented more than 5,000 performances during the Vietnam War featuring stars such as John Wayne, Ann-Margret, Sammy Davis Jr., Phyllis Diller, Martha Raye, Joey Heatherton, Wayne Newton, Jayne Mansfield, Redd Foxx, Rosey Grier, Anita Bryant, Nancy Sinatra, Jimmy Boyd, Lola Falana, and (of course) Bob Hope. Even Philip Ahn, the first actor of Korean descent to become a Hollywood star, became the first Asian American USO performer to entertain troops in Vietnam.

In addition, the USO operated centers at major U.S. airports to provide a lounge and place to sleep for American servicemen between their flights. Vietnam historian James Westheider noted that the USO "tried to bring a little America to Vietnam." Volunteer American civilians, who did 18-month tours, staffed the clubs. According to Westheider, "The young women wore miniskirts - no slacks were allowed." Each club had a snack bar, gift shops, a barbershop, photo developing, overseas phone lines, and hot showers.

When providing entertainment, the USO did its best to attract known stars from back home to help relieve the stresses of war. Even Senator John Kerry recalled how important this kind of diversion would become. He remembered a "Bob Hope Follies" USO show, which included actress Ann Margret, Miss America, football star Rosey Grier, and others. According to Kerry biographer Douglas Brinkley, "When the Swift finally made it back to the My Tho River, the crew confronted the heartbreaking sight of a huge Navy landing craft ferrying the troops back. The USO show was over." Kerry later wrote, "The visions of Ann Margret and Miss America and all the other titillating personalities who would have made us feel so at home hung around us for a while until we saw three Chinook helicopters take off from the field and presumed that our dreams had gone with them."

But for GIs who saw the show, it was worth it: "We turned to watch Ann perform, and for about two minutes of American beauty, the war was forgotten. Everyone fully understood just what was really worth fighting for. . . . The show was fantastic, but the escape the Bob Hope tour provided us in expectation for days before, and after, helped us keep in touch with what we were there for -- God, Country, apple pie ... and Ann-Margret!"

The visits by the stars meant a lot to the men and women in Vietnam. "It was not just the entertainment; it meant that they were not forgotten that far away from home," writes Westheider. He adds that the tours made a "deep impression" on the stars as well. Singer and actress Connie Stevens remembered her 1969 tour with Bob Hope, when she decided to go despite the fact she had two children both under the age of two. Today, she claims that "veterans were still stopping her and thanking her for visiting Vietnam over 30 years later."

Afghanistan and Iraq

To support troops participating in Operations Enduring Freedom and Iraqi Freedom, USO centers opened in Afghanistan, Iraq, Kuwait and Qatar. USO centers number more than 130 around the world. Recently, the USO opened the Rocky Mountain USO Center at Denver International Airport, a third center in Kuwait and its first center in Iraq at Balad Air Base. The USO provides a variety of programs and services, including orientation programs, family events, travel assistance, free Internet and e-mail access, and recreation services. A new program called "USO in a Box," delivers program materials ranging from DVD players and videos to musical instruments to remote forward operating bases in Afghanistan and Iraq.

U.S. military personnel and their families visit USO centers more than five million times each year.

From June 8 to 11, 2009, T.V. personality Stephen Colbert traveled to Iraq to film his show *The Colbert Report* for four days in a USO sponsored event.

Other entertainers who have traveled to Iraq, Kuwait and Afghanistan to perform include Gary Sinise, Carrie Underwood, Drowning Pool, Toby Keith, Montgomery Gentry, Kellie Pickler, Carlos Mencia, O.A.R., Dave Attell, Trace Adkins, Louis C.K., Dane Cook, Third Day, and Neil McCoy.

The USO is also providing services for the annual "Tribute to the Troops" special of World Wrestling Entertainment. They have aired WWE RAW from Afghanistan and Iraq every Christmas in the United States in a pre-taped show from the combat zone.

Honoring Bob Hope

In 1996, the U.S. Congress honored Bob Hope by declaring him the "first and only honorary veteran of the U.S. armed forces." According to Hope biographer William Faith, his reputation has become ingrained in the "American consciousness" because he had flown millions of miles to entertain G.I.s during both wartime and peace. His contribution to the USO began in 1941 and ended with Operation Desert Shield in 1991. He was always treated as "an asset to the U.S. Government with his willingness to entertain whenever they needed him." After WWII was declared over, the USO had sent out an "impassioned bulletin" asking entertainers not to abandon the GIs now that the war was over. Hope was among the first to say "yes." The Military Order of the Purple Heart notes that "his contributions to the USO are well known: they are legend."

As a result of his non-stop entertainment to both the civilian population and the military, he received numerous other honors over the years: a C-17 Air Force plane was named *The Spirit of Bob Hope*; a naval vessel was named the *USNS Bob Hope*; and streets, schools, hospitals, and a golf tournament were also named in his honor. A Senate resolution declared him "a part of American folklore." The *Guinness Book of Records* called him the most honored entertainer ever. And during his 1993 televised birthday celebration, when he turned 90, General Colin Powell saluted Hope "for his tireless USO trouping", which was followed by onstage tributes from all branches of the armed forces. General William Westmoreland spoke about his loyalty to the GI throughout the gritty Vietnam years. And bandleader Les Brown, who was with him during many of his tours, mentioned that his band "had seen more of Hope's ass in the last forty years than any of Hope's immediate family."

War correspondent Quentin Reynolds wrote in 1943, "He and his troupe would do 300 miles in a jeep, and give four shows . . . . One of the generals said Hope was a first rate military target since he was worth a division; that that's about 15,000 men. Presumably the Nazis appreciated Hope's value, since they thrice bombed towns while the comic was there."

During the Vietnam war years he gave a number of high-rating television specials and sensed that the media had given him a broad endorsement for continuing on his GI mercy missions. Soon after his Christmas show in Saigon in 1967, he learned that the Vietcong had planned a terrorist attack at his hotel against him and his entire troupe, missing him by ten minutes. He was later "mystified," writes Faith, "and ... increasingly intolerant of the pockets of dissent. Draft-card burnings on college campuses angered him..." "Can you imagine," Hope wrote in a magazine article, "... that people in America are burning their draft cards to show their opposition and that some of them are actually rooting for your defeat?" In the spring of 1973, Hope began writing his fifth book, *The Last Christmas Show*, which was dedicated to "the men and women of the armed forces and to those who also served by worrying and waiting." He signed over his royalties to the USO.

His final Christmas show was during Operation Desert Shield in 1990. The show was not easy, notes Faith. "There were so many restrictions. Hope's jokes were monitored by the State Department to avoid offending the Saudis. . . . and the media was restricted from covering the shows. . . . Because in Saudi Arabia national custom prescribes that women must be veiled in public, Ann Jillian, Marie Osmond, and the Pointer Sisters were left off Hope's Christmas Eve show."

In 2009, Stephen Colbert performing his last episode of week-long taping for his The Colbert Report show, carried a golf club on stage and dedicated it to Bob Hope's service for the USO.

Financials

The USO has a paid staff of approximately 240. Additionally, more than 30,000 USO volunteers provide an estimated 371,417 hours of service annually. As reported by the USO, the unpaid volunteer to paid employee ratio overseas is 20 to 1. Within the United States, the number is "significantly higher".

The following information is based on USO's audited financial statements for the year ended December 31, 2006:

Source of Funds	U.S. $
In-kind contributions	83,497,430
Public appeals	32,325,150
USO center revenue	13,660,792
Corporate, foundation and individual giving	8,748,594
Investment income	6,440,121
Entertainment sponsorships	2,593,504
United Way, CFC and other federated	1,040,528
Rental and other income	393,703
Total Income	**148,699,822**

Expenses	U.S. $
Program expenses	124,008,404
Fund raising expenses	12,767,448
Administrative expenses	6,571,080
Total expenses	**143,346,932**

External links

- Official website [1]
- Other web site: USO Clubs in World War II [2]
- Movie clips: Re-enacted WWII tour [3], from *Jolson Sings Again* (1949)
- USO World Gala, 2008: President Bush speech [4] Text and video, Oct. 1, 2008

See Also

- United Service Organization of North Carolina

Red Cross

International Red Cross and Red Crescent Movement

The Red Cross and Red Crescent emblems, the symbols from which the movement derives its name.	
Founders	Henry Dunant
Founded	1863
Location	Geneva, Switzerland
Area served	Worldwide
Focus	Humanitarian
Method	Aid
Website	http://www.redcross.int/

The **International Red Cross and Red Crescent Movement** is an international humanitarian movement with approximately 97 million volunteers, members and staff worldwide which was founded to protect human life and health, to ensure respect for all human beings, and to prevent and alleviate human suffering, without any discrimination based on nationality, race, sex, religious beliefs, class or political opinions.

The often-heard term *International Red Cross* is actually a misnomer, as no official organization as such exists bearing that name. In reality, the movement consists of several distinct organizations that are legally independent from each other, but are united within the Movement through common basic principles, objectives, symbols, statutes and governing organs. The Movement's parts:

- The International Committee of the Red Cross (ICRC) is a private humanitarian institution founded in 1863 in Geneva, Switzerland, by Henry Dunant. Its 25-member committee has a unique authority under international humanitarian law to protect the life and dignity of the victims of international and internal armed conflicts. The ICRC was awarded the Nobel Peace Prize on three occasions (in 1917, 1944 and 1963).

- The International Federation of Red Cross and Red Crescent Societies (IFRC) was founded in 1919 and today it coordinates activities between the 186 National Red Cross and Red Crescent Societies within the Movement. On an international level, the Federation leads and organizes, in close cooperation with the National Societies, relief assistance missions responding to large-scale emergencies. The International Federation Secretariat is based in Geneva, Switzerland. In 1963, the Federation (then known as the League of Red Cross Societies) was awarded the Nobel Peace Prize jointly with the ICRC.

- National Red Cross and Red Crescent Societies exist in nearly every country in the world. Currently 186 National Societies are recognized by the ICRC and admitted as full members of the Federation. Each entity works in its home country according to the principles of international humanitarian law and the statutes of the international Movement. Depending on their specific circumstances and capacities, National Societies can take on additional humanitarian tasks that are not directly defined by international humanitarian law or the mandates of the international Movement. In many countries, they are tightly linked to the respective national health care system by providing emergency medical services.

History of Movement

The International Committee of the Red Cross

Solferino, Henry Dunant and the foundation of the ICRC

Until the middle of the 19th century, there were no organized and well-established army nursing systems for casualties and no safe and protected institutions to accommodate and treat those who were wounded on the battlefield. In June 1859, the Swiss businessman Henry Dunant traveled to Italy to meet French emperor Napoléon III with the intention of discussing difficulties in conducting business in Algeria, at that time occupied by France. When he arrived in the small town of Solferino on the evening of June 24, he witnessed the Battle of Solferino, an engagement in the Austro-Sardinian War. In a single day, about 40,000 soldiers on both sides died or were left wounded on the field. Henry Dunant was shocked by the terrible aftermath of the battle, the suffering of the wounded soldiers, and the near-total lack of medical attendance and basic care. He completely abandoned the original intent of his trip and for several days he devoted himself to helping with

Henry Dunant, author of "A Memory of Solferino"

the treatment and care for the wounded. He succeeded in organizing an overwhelming level of relief assistance by motivating the local population to aid without discrimination. Back in his home in Geneva, he decided to write a book entitled *A Memory of Solferino* which he published with his own money in 1862. He sent copies of the book to leading political and military figures throughout Europe. In addition to penning a vivid description of his experiences in Solferino in 1859, he explicitly advocated the formation of national voluntary relief organizations to help nurse wounded soldiers in the case of war. In addition, he called for the development of international treaties to guarantee the protection of neutral medics and field hospitals for soldiers wounded on the battlefield.

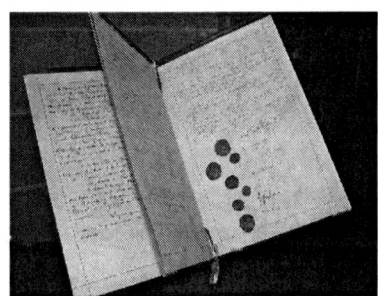

Original document of the first Geneva Convention, 1864

On February 9, 1863, in Geneva, Henry Dunant founded the "Committee of the Five" (together with four other leading figures from well-known Geneva families) as an investigatory commission of the Geneva Society for Public Welfare. Their aim was to examine the feasibility of Dunant's ideas and to organize an international conference about their possible implementation. The members of this committee, aside from Dunant himself, were Gustave Moynier, lawyer and chairman of the Geneva Society for Public Welfare; physician Louis Appia, who had significant experience working as a field surgeon; Appia's friend and colleague Théodore Maunoir, from the Geneva Hygiene and Health Commission; and Guillaume-Henri Dufour, a Swiss Army general of great renown. Eight days later, the five men decided to rename the committee to the

"International Committee for Relief to the Wounded". In October (26–29) 1863, the international conference organized by the committee was held in Geneva to develop possible measures to improve medical services on the battlefield. The conference was attended by 36 individuals: eighteen official delegates from national governments, six delegates from other non-governmental organizations, seven non-official foreign delegates, and the five members of the International Committee. The states and kingdoms represented by official delegates were:

- Austria
- Baden
- France
- Hesse-Kassel
- The Netherlands
- Prussia
- Russian Empire
- Spain
- Sweden-Norway

Among the proposals written in the final resolutions of the conference, adopted on October 29, 1863, were:

- The foundation of national relief societies for wounded soldiers;
- Neutrality and protection for wounded soldiers;
- The utilization of volunteer forces for relief assistance on the battlefield;
- The organization of additional conferences to enact these concepts in legally binding international treaties; and
- The introduction of a common distinctive protection symbol for medical personnel in the field, namely a white armlet bearing a red cross.

Only one year later, the Swiss government invited the governments of all European countries, as well as the United States, Brazil, and Mexico, to attend an official diplomatic conference. Sixteen countries sent a total of twenty-six delegates to Geneva. On August 22, 1864, the conference adopted the first Geneva Convention "for the Amelioration of the Condition of the Wounded in Armies in the Field". Representatives of 12 states and kingdoms signed the convention: Baden, Belgium, Denmark, France, Hesse, Italy, the Netherlands, Portugal, Prussia, Switzerland, Spain, and Württemberg. The convention contained ten articles, establishing for the first time legally binding rules guaranteeing neutrality and protection for wounded soldiers, field medical personnel, and specific humanitarian institutions in an armed conflict. Furthermore, the convention defined two specific requirements for recognition of a national relief society by the International Committee:

- The national society must be recognized by its own national government as a relief society according to the convention, and
- The national government of the respective country must be a state party to the Geneva Convention.

Directly following the establishment of the Geneva Convention, the first national societies were founded in Belgium, Denmark, France, Oldenburg, Prussia, Spain, and Württemberg. Also in 1864, Louis Appia and Charles van de Velde, a captain of the Dutch Army, became the first independent and neutral delegates to work under the symbol of the Red Cross in an armed conflict. Three years later in 1867, the first International Conference of National Aid Societies for the Nursing of the War Wounded was convened.

Also in 1867, Henry Dunant was forced to declare bankruptcy due to business failures in Algeria, partly because he had neglected his business interests during his tireless activities for the International Committee. Controversy surrounding Dunant's business dealings and the resulting negative public opinion, combined with an ongoing conflict with Gustave Moynier, led to Dunant's expulsion from his position as a member and secretary. He was charged with fraudulent bankruptcy and a warrant for his arrest was issued. Thus, he was forced to leave Geneva and never returned to his home city. In the following years, national societies were founded in nearly every country in Europe. In 1876, the committee adopted the name "International Committee of the Red Cross" (ICRC), which is still its official designation today. Five years later, the American Red Cross was founded through the efforts of Clara Barton. More and more countries signed the Geneva Convention and began to respect it in practice during armed conflicts. In a rather short period of time, the Red Cross gained huge momentum as an internationally respected movement, and the national societies became increasingly popular as a venue for volunteer work.

When the first Nobel Peace Prize was awarded in 1901, the Norwegian Nobel Committee opted to give it jointly to Henry Dunant and Frédéric Passy, a leading international pacifist. More significant than the honor of the prize itself, the official congratulation from the International Committee of the Red Cross marked the overdue rehabilitation of Henry Dunant and represented a tribute to his key role in the formation of the Red Cross. Dunant died nine years later in the small Swiss health resort of Heiden. Only two months earlier his long-standing adversary Gustave Moynier had also died, leaving a mark in the history of the Committee as its longest-serving president ever.

In 1906, the 1864 Geneva Convention was revised for the first time. One year later, the Hague Convention X, adopted at the Second International Peace Conference in The Hague, extended the scope of the Geneva Convention to naval warfare. Shortly before the beginning of the First World War in 1914, 50 years after the foundation of the ICRC and the adoption of the first Geneva Convention, there were already 45 national relief societies throughout the world. The movement had extended itself beyond Europe and North America to Central and South America (Argentina, Brazil, Chile, Cuba, Mexico, Peru, El Salvador, Uruguay, Venezuela), Asia (the Republic of China, Japan, Korea, Siam), and Africa (Republic of South Africa).

The ICRC during World War I

French postcard celebrating the role of Red Cross nurses during the First World War, 1915

Ernest Hemingway in uniform as a Red Cross ambulance driver

With the outbreak of World War I, the ICRC found itself confronted with enormous challenges that it could handle only by working closely with the national Red Cross societies. Red Cross nurses from around the world, including the United States and Japan, came to support the medical services of the armed forces of the European countries involved in the war. On October 15, 1914, immediately after the start of the war, the ICRC set up its International Prisoners-of-War (POW) Agency, which had about 1,200 mostly volunteer staff members by the end of 1914. By the end of the war, the Agency had transferred about 20 million letters and messages, 1.9 million parcels, and about 18 million Swiss francs in monetary donations to POWs of all affected countries. Furthermore, due to the intervention of the Agency, about 200,000 prisoners were exchanged between the warring parties, released from captivity and returned to their home country. The organizational card index of the Agency accumulated about 7 million records from 1914 to 1923, each card representing an individual prisoner or missing person. The card index led to the identification of about 2 million POWs and the ability to contact their families. The complete index is on loan today from the ICRC to the International Red Cross and Red Crescent Museum in Geneva. The right to access the index is still strictly restricted to the ICRC.

French war casualty wearing a prosthetic mask provided by the American Red Cross, 1918

The same man without his mask

During the entire war, the ICRC monitored warring parties' compliance with the Geneva Conventions of the 1907 revision and forwarded complaints about violations to the respective country. When chemical weapons were used in this war for the first time in history, the ICRC vigorously protested against this new type of warfare. Even without having a mandate from the Geneva Conventions, the ICRC tried to ameliorate the suffering of civil populations. In territories that were officially designated as "occupied territories," the ICRC could assist the civilian population on the basis of the Hague Convention's "Laws and Customs of War on Land" of 1907. This convention was also the legal basis for the ICRC's work for prisoners of war. In addition to the work of the International Prisoner-of-War Agency as described above this included inspection visits to POW camps. A total of 524 camps throughout Europe were visited by 41 delegates from the ICRC until the end of the war.

Between 1916 and 1918, the ICRC published a number of postcards with scenes from the POW camps. The pictures showed the prisoners in day-to-day activities such as the distribution of letters from home. The intention of the ICRC was to provide the families of the prisoners with some hope and solace and to alleviate their uncertainties about the fate of their loved ones. After the end of the war, the ICRC organized the return of about 420,000 prisoners to their home countries. In 1920, the task of repatriation was handed over to the newly founded League of Nations, which appointed the Norwegian diplomat and scientist Fridtjof Nansen as its "High Commissioner for Repatriation of the War Prisoners." His legal mandate was later extended to support and care for war refugees and displaced persons when his office became that of the League of Nations "High Commissioner for Refugees." Nansen, who invented the *Nansen passport* for stateless refugees and was awarded the Nobel Peace Prize in 1922, appointed two delegates from the ICRC as his deputies.

A year before the end of the war, the ICRC received the 1917 Nobel Peace Prize for its outstanding wartime work. It was the only Nobel Peace Prize awarded in the period from 1914 to 1918. In 1923, the Committee adopted a change in its policy regarding the selection of new members. Until then, only citizens from the city of Geneva could serve in the Committee. This limitation was expanded to include Swiss citizens. As a direct consequence of World War I, an additional protocol to the Geneva Convention was adopted in 1925 which outlawed the use of suffocating or poisonous gases and biological agents as weapons. Four years later, the original Convention was revised and the second Geneva Convention "relative to the Treatment of Prisoners of War" was established. The events of World War I and the respective activities of the ICRC significantly increased the reputation and authority of the Committee among the international community and led to an extension of its competencies.

As early as in 1934, a draft proposal for an additional convention for the protection of the civil population during an armed conflict was adopted by the International Red Cross Conference. Unfortunately, most governments had little interest in implementing this convention, and it was thus prevented from entering into force before the beginning of World War II.

The ICRC and World War II

The legal basis of the work of the ICRC during World War II were the Geneva Conventions in their 1929 revision. The activities of the Committee were similar to those during World War I: visiting and monitoring POW camps, organizing relief assistance for civilian populations, and administering the exchange of messages regarding prisoners and missing persons. By the end of the war, 179 delegates had conducted 12,750 visits to POW camps in 41 countries. The Central Information Agency on Prisoners-of-War (*Zentralauskunftsstelle für Kriegsgefangene*) had a staff of 3,000, the card index tracking prisoners contained 45 million cards, and 120 million messages were exchanged by the Agency.

Red Cross message from Łódź, Poland, 1940.

One major obstacle was that the Nazi-controlled German Red Cross refused to cooperate with the Geneva statutes including blatant violations such as the deportation of Jews from Germany and the mass murders conducted in the Nazi concentration camps. Moreover, two other main parties to the conflict, the Soviet Union and Japan, were not party to the 1929 Geneva Conventions and were not legally required to follow the rules of the conventions.

During the war, the ICRC was unable to obtain an agreement with Nazi Germany about the treatment of detainees in concentration camps, and it eventually abandoned applying pressure in order to avoid disrupting its work with POWs. The ICRC was also unable to obtain a response to reliable information about the extermination camps and the mass killing of European Jews, Roma, et al. After November 1943, the ICRC achieved permission to send parcels to concentration camp detainees with known names and locations. Because the notices of receipt for these parcels were often signed by other inmates, the ICRC managed to register the identities of about 105,000 detainees in the concentration camps and delivered about 1.1 million parcels, primarily to the camps Dachau, Buchenwald, Ravensbrück, and Sachsenhausen.

It is known that Swiss army officer Maurice Rossel during World War II had been sent to Berlin as a delegate of the International Red Cross, as such he visited Auschwitz 1943 and Theresienstadt 1944. Claude Lanzmann recorded his experiences in 1979, producing a documentary entitled *Visitor from the living.*

Marcel Junod, delegate of the ICRC, visiting POWs in Germany.
(© Benoit Junod, Switzerland)

On March 12, 1945, ICRC president Jacob Burckhardt received a message from SS General Ernst Kaltenbrunner accepting the ICRC's demand to allow delegates to visit the concentration camps. This agreement was bound by the condition that these delegates would have to stay in the camps until the end of the war. Ten delegates, among them Louis Haefliger (Camp Mauthausen), Paul Dunant (Camp Theresienstadt) and Victor Maurer (Camp Dachau), accepted the assignment and visited the camps. Louis Haefliger prevented the forceful eviction or blasting of Mauthausen-Gusen by alerting American troops, thereby saving the lives of about 60,000 inmates. His actions were condemned by the ICRC because they were deemed as acting unduly on his own authority and risking the ICRC's neutrality. Only in 1990, his reputation was finally rehabilitated by ICRC president Cornelio Sommaruga.

Another example of great humanitarian spirit was Friedrich Born (1903–1963), an ICRC delegate in Budapest who saved the lives of about 11,000 to 15,000 Jewish people in Hungary. Marcel Junod (1904–1961), a physician from Geneva, was another famous delegate during the Second World War. An account of his experiences, which included being one of the first foreigners to visit Hiroshima after the atomic bomb was dropped, can be found in the book *Warrior without Weapons*.

In 1944, the ICRC received its second Nobel Peace Prize. As in World War I, it received the only Peace Prize awarded during the main period of war, 1939 to 1945. At the end of the war, the ICRC worked with national Red Cross societies to organize relief assistance to those countries most severely affected. In 1948, the Committee published a report reviewing its war-era activities from September 1, 1939 to June 30, 1947. Since January 1996, the ICRC archive for this period has been open to academic and public research.

The ICRC after the Second World War

On August 12, 1949, further revisions to the existing two Geneva Conventions were adopted. An additional convention "for the Amelioration of the Condition of Wounded, Sick and Shipwrecked Members of Armed Forces at Sea", now called the second Geneva Convention, was brought under the Geneva Convention umbrella as a successor to the 1907 Hague Convention X. The 1929 Geneva convention "relative to the Treatment of Prisoners of War" may have been the second Geneva Convention from a historical point of view (because it was actually formulated in Geneva), but after 1949 it came to be called the third Convention because it came later chronologically than the Hague Convention. Reacting to the experience of World War II, the Fourth Geneva Convention, a new Convention "relative to the Protection of Civilian Persons in Time of War," was established. Also, the additional protocols of June 8, 1977 were intended to make the conventions apply to internal conflicts such as civil wars. Today, the four conventions and their added protocols contain more than 600 articles, a remarkable expansion when compared to the mere 10 articles in the first 1864 convention.

The ICRC Headquarters in Geneva

In celebration of its centennial in 1963, the ICRC, together with the League of Red Cross Societies, received its third Nobel Peace Prize. Since 1993, non-Swiss individuals have been allowed to serve as Committee delegates abroad, a task which was previously restricted to Swiss citizens. Indeed, since then, the share of staff without Swiss citizenship has increased to about 35%.

On October 16, 1990, the UN General Assembly decided to grant the ICRC observer status for its assembly sessions and sub-committee meetings, the first observer status given to a private organization. The resolution was jointly proposed by 138 member states and introduced by the Italian ambassador, Vieri Traxler, in memory of the organization's origins in the Battle of Solferino. An agreement with the Swiss government signed on March 19, 1993, affirmed the already long-standing policy of full independence of the Committee from any possible interference by Switzerland. The agreement protects the full sanctity of all ICRC property in Switzerland including its headquarters and archive, grants members and staff legal immunity, exempts the ICRC from all taxes and fees, guarantees the protected and duty-free transfer of goods, services, and money, provides the ICRC with secure communication privileges at the same level as foreign embassies, and simplifies Committee travel in and out of Switzerland.

At the end of the Cold War, the ICRC's work actually became more dangerous. In the 1990s, more delegates lost their lives than at any point in its history, especially when working in local and internal armed conflicts. These incidents often demonstrated a lack of respect for the rules of the Geneva Conventions and their protection symbols. Among the slain delegates were:

- Frédéric Maurice. He died on May 19, 1992 at the age of 39, one day after a Red Cross transport he was escorting was attacked in the Bosnian city of Sarajevo.
- Fernanda Calado (Spain), Ingeborg Foss (Norway), Nancy Malloy (Canada), Gunnhild Myklebust (Norway), Sheryl Thayer (New Zealand), and Hans Elkerbout (Netherlands). They were murdered at point-blank range while sleeping in the early hours of December 17, 1996 in the ICRC field hospital in the Chechen city of Nowije Atagi near Grozny. Their murderers have never been caught and there was no apparent motive for the killings.
- Rita Fox (Switzerland), Véronique Saro (Democratic Republic of Congo, formerly Zaire), Julio Delgado (Colombia), Unen Ufoirworth (DR Congo), Aduwe Boboli (DR Congo), and Jean Molokabonge (DR Congo). On April 26, 2001, they were en route with two cars on a relief mission in the northeast of the Democratic Republic of Congo when they came under fatal fire from unknown attackers.
- Ricardo Munguia (El Salvador). He was working as a water engineer in Afghanistan and travelling with local colleagues when their car on March 27, 2003 was stopped by unknown armed men. He was killed execution-style at point-blank range while his colleagues were allowed to escape. He died at the age of 39.
- Vatche Arslanian (Canada). Since 2001, he worked as a logistics coordinator for the ICRC mission in Iraq. He died when he was travelling through Baghdad together with members of the Iraqi Red Crescent. On April 8, 2003 their car accidentally came into the cross fire of fighting in the city.
- Nadisha Yasassri Ranmuthu (Sri Lanka). He was killed by unknown attackers on July 22, 2003 when his car was fired upon near the city of Hilla in the south of Baghdad.

Afghanistan

ICRC is active in the Afghanistan conflict areas and has set up six physical rehabilitation centers to help landmine victims. Their support extends to the national and international armed forces, civilians and the armed opposition. They have provided basic first aid training and aid kits to Taliban members as well because, according to an ICRC spokesperson, "ICRC's constitution stipulates that all parties harmed by warfare will be treated as fairly as possible".[1]

The International Federation of Red Cross and Red Crescent Societies

History

In 1919, representatives from the national Red Cross societies of Britain, France, Italy, Japan, and the US came together in Paris to found the "League of Red Cross Societies". The original idea was Henry Davison's, then president of the American Red Cross. This move, led by the American Red Cross, expanded the international activities of the Red Cross movement beyond the strict mission of the ICRC to include relief assistance in response to emergency situations which were not caused by war (such as man-made or natural disasters). The ARC already had great disaster relief mission experience extending back to its foundation.

Henry Davison, Founding father of the League of Red Cross societies.
(Picture from: www.redcross.int [2])

The formation of the League, as an additional international Red Cross organization alongside the ICRC, was not without controversy for a number of reasons. The ICRC had, to some extent, valid concerns about a possible rivalry between both organizations. The foundation of the League was seen as an attempt to undermine the leadership position of the ICRC within the movement and to gradually transfer most of its tasks and competencies to a multilateral institution. In addition to that, all founding members of the League were national societies from countries of the Entente or from associated partners of the Entente. The original statutes of the League from May 1919 contained further regulations which gave the five founding societies a privileged status and, due to the efforts of Henry P. Davison, the right to permanently exclude the national Red Cross societies from the countries of the Central Powers, namely Germany, Austria, Hungary, Bulgaria and Turkey, and in addition to that the national Red Cross society of Russia. These rules were contrary to the Red Cross principles of universality and equality among all national societies, a situation which furthered the concerns of the ICRC.

The first relief assistance mission organized by the League was an aid mission for the victims of a famine and subsequent typhus epidemic in Poland. Only five years after its foundation, the League had already issued 47 donation appeals for missions in 34 countries, an impressive indication of the need for this type of Red Cross work. The total sum raised by these appeals reached 685 million Swiss Francs, which were used to bring emergency supplies to the victims of famines in Russia, Germany, and Albania; earthquakes in Chile, Persia, Japan, Colombia, Ecuador, Costa Rica, and Turkey; and refugee flows in Greece and Turkey. The first large-scale disaster mission of the League came after the 1923 earthquake in Japan which killed about 200,000 people and left countless more wounded and without shelter. Due to the League's coordination, the Red Cross society of Japan received goods from its sister societies reaching a total worth of about $100 million. Another important new field initiated by the League was the creation of youth Red Cross organizations within the national societies.

A joint mission of the ICRC and the League in the Russian Civil War from 1917 to 1922 marked the first time the movement was involved in an internal conflict, although still without an explicit mandate from the Geneva Conventions. The League, with support from more than 25 national societies, organized assistance missions and the distribution of food and other aid goods for civil populations affected by hunger and disease. The ICRC worked with the Russian Red Cross society and later the society of the Soviet Union, constantly emphasizing the ICRC's neutrality. In 1928, the "International Council" was founded to coordinate cooperation between the ICRC and the League, a task which was later taken over by the "Standing Commission". In the same year, a common statute for the movement was adopted for the first time, defining the respective roles of the ICRC and the League within the movement.

During the Abyssinian war between Ethiopia and Italy from 1935 to 1936, the League contributed aid supplies worth about 1.7 million Swiss Francs. Because the Italian fascist regime under Benito Mussolini refused any cooperation with the Red Cross, these goods were delivered solely to Ethiopia. During the war, an estimated 29 people lost their lives while being under explicit protection of the Red Cross symbol, most of them due to attacks by the Italian Army. During the Civil War in Spain from 1936 to 1939 the League once again joined forces with the ICRC with the support of 41 national societies. In 1939 on the brink of the Second World War, the League relocated its headquarters from Paris to Geneva to take advantage of Swiss neutrality.

Peace Nobel Prize ceremony in 1963; From left to right: Crown Prince Harald of Norway, King Olav of Norway, ICRC President Leopold Boissier, League Chairman John A. MacAulay. (Picture from: www.redcross.int [2])

In 1952, the 1928 common statute of the movement was revised for the first time. Also, the period of decolonization from 1960 to 1970 was marked by a huge jump in the number of recognized national Red Cross and Red Crescent societies. By the end of the 1960s, there were more than 100 societies around the world. On December 10, 1963, the Federation and the ICRC received the Nobel Peace Prize. In 1983, the League was renamed to the "League of Red Cross and Red Crescent Societies" to reflect the growing number of national societies operating under the Red Crescent symbol. Three years later, the seven basic principles of the movement as adopted in 1965 were incorporated into its statutes. The name of the League was changed again in 1991 to its current official designation the "International Federation of Red Cross and Red Crescent Societies". In 1997, the ICRC and the Federation signed the Seville Agreement which further defined the responsibilities of both organizations within the movement. In 2004, the Federation began its largest mission to date after the tsunami disaster in South Asia. More than 40 national societies have worked with more than 22,000 volunteers to bring relief to the countless victims left without food and shelter and endangered by the risk of epidemics.

Presidents of the Federation

As of November 2009, the president of the IFRC is Tadateru Konoe (Japanese Red Cross). The vice presidents are Paul Bierch (Kenya), Jaslin Uriah Salmon (Jamaica), Mohamed El Maadid (Qatar) and Bengt Westerberg (Sweden).

Former presidents (until 1977 titled "Chairman") have been:

- 1919–1922: Henry Davison (United States)
- 1922–1935: John Barton Payne (U.S.)
- 1935–1938: Cary Travers Grayson (U.S.)
- 1938–1944: Norman Davis (U.S.)
- 1944–1945: Jean de Muralt (Switzerland)
- 1945–1950: Basil O'Connor (U.S.)
- 1950–1959: Emil Sandström (Sweden)
- 1959–1965: John MacAulay (Canada)
- 1965–1977: José Barroso Chávez (Mexico)
- 1977–1981: Adetunji Adefarasin (Nigeria)
- 1981–1987: Enrique de la Mata (Spain)
- 1987–1997: Mario Enrique Villarroel Lander (Venezuela)
- 1997–2000: Astrid Nøklebye Heiberg (Norway)
- 2001 - 2009: Juan Manuel del Toro y Rivera (Spain)
- 2009 - : Tadateru Konoé (Japan)

World Red Cross Red Crescent Day – 8 May

May 8, birthday of Henry Dunant, founder of the Red Cross, is celebrated as the World Red Cross and Red Crescent Day.

World Red Cross Red Crescent Day 2010

On the occasion of the World Red Cross Red Crescent Day 2010, the International Red Cross and Red Crescent Movement focused its attention on both the challenges and opportunities presented by urbanization. Around the world, National Red Cross and Red Crescent Societies are working with city leaders and civil society to address urban challenges by aiming at their root causes. They focus on promoting diversity, opposing discrimination, and joining in efforts to provide decent social services and to ensure that adequate protection, preventive health-care, education and disaster risk reduction measures are taken.

Activities

Organization of the Movement

Altogether, there are about 97 million people worldwide who serve with the ICRC, the International Federation, and the National Societies.

The 1965 International Conference in Vienna adopted seven basic principles which should be shared by all parts of the Movement, and they were added to the official statutes of the Movement in 1986.

- Humanity
- Impartiality
- Neutrality
- Independence
- Voluntary Service
- Unity
- Universality

Entry to the International Red Cross and Red Crescent Museum in Geneva.

The International Red Cross and Red Crescent Conference, which occurs once every four years, is the highest institutional body of the Movement. It gathers delegations from all of the national societies as well as from the ICRC, the Federation and the signatory states to the Geneva Conventions. In between the conferences, the Standing Commission acts as the supreme body and supervises implementation of and compliance with the resolutions of the conference. In addition, the Standing Commission coordinates the cooperation between the ICRC and the Federation. It consists of two representatives from the ICRC (including its president), two from the Federation (including its president), and five individuals who are elected by the International Conference. The Standing Commission convenes every six months on average. Moreover, a convention of the Council of Delegates of the Movement takes place every two years in the course of the conferences of the General Assemblies of the Federation. The Council of Delegates plans and coordinates joint activities for the Movement.

Activities and Organization of the ICRC

The mission of the ICRC and its responsibilities within the Movement

The official mission of the ICRC as an impartial, neutral, and independent organization is to stand for the protection of the life and dignity of victims of international and internal armed conflicts. According to the 1997 Seville Agreement, it is the "Lead Agency" of the Movement in conflicts. The core tasks of the Committee, which are derived from the Geneva Conventions and its own statutes, are the following:

- to monitor compliance of warring parties with the Geneva Conventions
- to organize nursing and care for those who are wounded on the battlefield
- to supervise the treatment of prisoners of war
- to help with the search for missing persons in an armed conflict (tracing service)
- to organize protection and care for civil populations
- to arbitrate between warring parties in an armed conflict

Emblem of the ICRC

Legal status and organization

The ICRC is headquartered in the Swiss city of Geneva and has external offices in about 80 countries. It has about 12,000 staff members worldwide, about 800 of them working in its Geneva headquarters, 1,200 expatriates with about half of them serving as delegates managing its international missions and the other half being specialists like doctors, agronomists, engineers or interpreters, and about 10,000 members of individual national societies working on site. Contrary to popular belief, the ICRC is not a non-governmental organization in the most common sense of the term, nor is it an international organization. As it limits its members (a process called cooptation) to Swiss nationals only, it does not have a policy of open and unrestricted membership for individuals like other legally defined NGOs. The word "international" in its name does not refer to its membership but to the worldwide scope of its activities as defined by the Geneva Conventions. The ICRC has special privileges and legal immunities in many countries, based on national law in these countries or through agreements between the Committee and respective national governments. According to Swiss law, the ICRC is defined as a private association. According to its statutes it consists of 15 to 25 Swiss-citizen members, which it coopts for a period of four years. There is no limit to the number of terms an individual member can have although a three-quarters majority of all members is required for re-election after the third term.

The leading organs of the ICRC are the Directorate and the Assembly. The Directorate is the executive body of the Committee. It consists of a General Director and five directors in the areas of "Operations",

"Human Resources", "Resources and Operational Support", "Communication", and "International Law and Cooperation within the Movement". The members of the Directorate are appointed by the Assembly to serve for four years. The Assembly, consisting of all of the members of the Committee, convenes on a regular basis and is responsible for defining aims, guidelines, and strategies and for supervising the financial matters of the Committee. The president of the Assembly is also the president of the Committee as a whole. Furthermore, the Assembly elects a five member Assembly Council which has the authority to decide on behalf of the full Assembly in some matters. The Council is also responsible for organizing the Assembly meetings and for facilitating communication between the Assembly and the Directorate.

Due to Geneva's location in the French-speaking part of Switzerland, the ICRC usually acts under its French name *Comité international de la Croix-Rouge* (CICR). The official symbol of the ICRC is the Red Cross on white background with the words "COMITE INTERNATIONAL GENEVE" circling the cross.

Funding and financial matters

The 2009 budget of the ICRC amounts more than 1 billon Swiss Francs. Most of that money comes from the States, including Switzerland in its capacity as the depositary state of the Geneva Conventions, from national Red Cross societies, the signatory states of the Geneva Conventions, and from international organizations like the European Union. All payments to the ICRC are voluntary and are received as donations based on two types of appeals issued by the Committee: an annual *Headquarters Appeal* to cover its internal costs and *Emergency Appeals* for its individual missions.

The ICRC is asking donors for more than 1.1 billion Swiss francs to fund its work in 2010. Afghanistan is projected to become the ICRC's biggest humanitarian operation (at 86 million Swiss francs, an 18% increase over the initial 2009 budget), followed by Iraq (85 million francs) and Sudan (76 million francs). The initial 2010 field budget for medical activities of 132 million francs represents an increase of 12 million francs over 2009.

Activities and organization of the Federation

The Mission of the Federation and its responsibilities within the Movement

The Federation coordinates cooperation between national Red Cross and Red Crescent societies throughout the world and supports the foundation of new national societies in countries where no official society exists. On the international stage, the Federation organizes and leads relief assistance missions after emergencies like natural disasters, manmade disasters, epidemics, mass refugee flights, and other emergencies. According to the 1997 Seville Agreement, the Federation is

Emblem of the Federation

the Lead Agency of the Movement in any emergency situation which does not take place as part of an armed conflict. The Federation cooperates with the national societies of those countries affected – each called the *Operating National Society* (ONS) – as well as the national societies of other countries willing to offer assistance – called *Participating National Societies* (PNS). Among the 187 national societies admitted to the General Assembly of the Federation as full members or observers, about 25–30 regularly work as PNS in other countries. The most active of those are the American Red Cross, the British Red Cross, the German Red Cross, and the Red Cross societies of Sweden and Norway. Another major mission of the Federation which has gained attention in recent years is its commitment to work towards a codified, worldwide ban on the use of land mines and to bring medical, psychological, and social support for people injured by land mines.

The tasks of the Federation can therefore be summarized as follows:

- to promote humanitarian principles and values
- to provide relief assistance in emergency situations of large magnitude
- to support the national societies with disaster preparedness through the education of voluntary members and the provision of equipment and relief supplies
- to support local health care projects
- to support the national societies with youth-related activities

Legal status and organization

Like the ICRC, the Federation has its headquarters in Geneva. It also runs 14 permanent regional offices and has about 350 delegates in more than 60 delegations around the world. The legal basis for the work of the Federation is its constitution. The executive body of the Federation is a secretariat, led by a Secretary General. The secretariat is supported by four divisions labeled "Support Services", "National Society and Field Support", "Policy and Relations" and "Movement Cooperation". The Movement Cooperation division organizes interaction and cooperation with the ICRC. The highest body of the Federation is the General Assembly which convenes every two years with delegates from all of the national societies. Among other tasks, the General Assembly elects the Secretary General. Between the convening of General Assemblies, the Governing Board is the leading body of the Federation. It has the authority to make decisions for the Federation in a number of areas. The

Governing Board consists of the president and the vice presidents of the Federation, the chairman of the Finance Commission, and twenty elected representatives from national societies. It is supported by four additional commissions: "Disaster Relief", "Youth", "Health & Community Services", and "Development".

The symbol of the Federation is the combination of the Red Cross (left) and Red Crescent (right) on a white background (surrounded by a red rectangular frame) without any additional text.

Funding and financial matters

The main parts of the budget of the Federation are funded by contributions from the national societies which are members of the Federation and through revenues from its investments. The exact amount of contributions from each member society is established by the Finance Commission and approved by the General Assembly. Any additional funding, especially for unforeseen expenses for relief assistance missions, is raised by appeals published by the Federation and comes from voluntary donations by national societies, governments, other organizations, corporations, and individuals.

National societies within the Movement

Official Recognition of a national society

National Red Cross and Red Crescent societies exist in nearly every country in the world. Within their home country, they take on the duties and responsibilities of a national relief society as defined by International Humanitarian Law. Within the Movement, the ICRC is responsible for legally recognizing a relief society as an official national Red Cross or Red Crescent society. The exact rules for recognition are defined in the statutes of the Movement. Article 4 of these statutes contains the *"Conditions for recognition of National Societies"*

> *In order to be recognized in terms of Article 5, paragraph 2 b) as a National Society, the Society shall meet the following conditions:*

1. *Be constituted on the territory of an independent State where the Geneva Convention for the Amelioration of the Condition of the Wounded and Sick in Armed Forces in the Field is in force.*
2. *Be the only National Red Cross or Red Crescent Society of the said State and be directed by a central body which shall alone be competent to represent it in its dealings with other components of the Movement.*
3. *Be duly recognized by the legal government of its country on the basis of the Geneva Conventions and of the national legislation as a voluntary aid society, auxiliary to the public authorities in the humanitarian field.*
4. *Have an autonomous status which allows it to operate in conformity with the Fundamental Principles of the Movement.*
5. *Use the name and emblem of the Red Cross or Red Crescent in conformity with the Geneva Conventions.*

6. *Be so organized as to be able to fulfill the tasks defined in its own statutes, including the preparation in peace time for its statutory tasks in case of armed conflict.*
7. *Extend its activities to the entire territory of the State.*
8. *Recruit its voluntary members and its staff without consideration of race, sex, class, religion or political opinions.*
9. *Adhere to the present Statutes, share in the fellowship which unites the components of the Movement and co-operate with them.*
10. *Respect the Fundamental Principles of the Movement and be guided in its work by the principles of international humanitarian law.*

After recognition by the ICRC, a national society is admitted as a member to the International Federation of Red Cross and Red Crescent societies.However some National Societies have severely objected to the recognition and admission process by claiming its unfair execution by ICRC and IFRC

Activities of national societies on a national and international stage

Despite formal independence regarding its organizational structure and work, each national society is still bound by the laws of its home country. In many countries, national Red Cross and Red Crescent societies enjoy exceptional privileges due to agreements with their governments or specific "Red Cross Laws" granting full independence as required by the International Movement. The duties and responsibilities of a national society as defined by International Humanitarian Law and the statutes of the Movement include humanitarian aid in armed conflicts and emergency crises such as natural disasters. Depending on their respective human, technical, financial, and organizational resources, many national societies take on additional humanitarian tasks within their home countries such as Blood donation services or acting as civilian Emergency Medical Service (EMS) providers. The ICRC and the International Federation cooperate with the national societies in their international missions, especially with human, material, and financial resources and organizing on-site logistics.

History of the emblems

For more details on this topic, see Emblems of the International Red Cross and Red Crescent Movement.

Emblems in use

The Red Cross

The **Red Cross** emblem was officially approved in Geneva in 1863.

The Red Cross flag is not to be confused with the St George's Cross which is on the flag of England, Barcelona, Freiburg, and several other places. In order to avoid this confusion the protected symbol is sometimes referred to as the "Greek Red Cross"; that term is also used in United States law to describe the Red Cross. The red cross of the St George cross extends to the edge of the flag, whereas the red cross on the Red Cross flag does not.

The flag of Switzerland, from which the original Red Cross is said to have been derived

The Red Cross flag is often confused with the Flag of Switzerland which is the opposite of it. In 1906, to put an end to the argument of Turkey that the flag took its roots from Christianity, it was decided to promote officially the idea that the Red Cross flag had been formed by reversing the federal colours of Switzerland, although no clear evidence of this origin had ever been found.

The Red Crescent

The **Red Crescent** emblem was first used by ICRC volunteers during the armed conflict between the Ottoman Empire and Russia (1877–1878). The symbol was officially adopted in 1929, and so far 33 Islamic states have recognized it.

The Red Crystal

On December 8, 2005, partly in response to growing pressure to accommodate Magen David Adom as a full member of the Red Cross & Red Crescent movement,[citation needed] a new emblem (officially the **Third Protocol Emblem,** but more commonly known as the **Red Crystal**) was adopted by an amendment of the Geneva Conventions known as Protocol III.

Recognized emblems in disuse

The Red Lion and Sun

The **Red Lion and Sun Society of Iran** was established in 1922 and admitted to the Red Cross & Red Crescent movement in 1923. However, some report the symbol was introduced at Geneva in 1864 [citation needed] as a counter example to the crescent and cross used by two of Iran's rivals, the Ottoman and the Russian empires. Though that claim is inconsistent with the Red Crescent's history, that history also suggests that the Red Lion and Sun, like the Red Crescent, may have been conceived during the 1877-1878 war between Russia and Turkey.

In 1980, because of the association of the emblem with the Shah, the newly proclaimed Islamic Republic of Iran replaced the Red Lion and Sun with the Red Crescent, consistent with most other Muslim nations. Though the Red Lion and Sun has now fallen into disuse, Iran has in the past reserved the right to take it up again at any time; the Geneva Conventions continue to recognize it as an official emblem, and that status was confirmed by Protocol III in 2005 even as it added the Red Crystal.[citation needed]

Unrecognized emblems

The Red Star of David (Magen David Adom)

For over 50 years, Israel requested the addition of a red Star of David, arguing that since Christian and Muslim emblems were recognized, the corresponding Jewish emblem should be as well. This emblem has been used since 1935 by Magen David Adom (MDA), or Red Star of David, the national first-aid society of Israel, but it is still not recognized by the Geneva Conventions as a protected symbol.

The Red Cross & Red Crescent movement repeatedly rejected Israel's request over the years, stating that the Red Cross emblem was not meant to represent Christianity but was a color reversal of the Swiss flag, and also that if Jews (or another group) were to be given another emblem, there would be no end to the number of religious or other groups claiming an emblem for themselves, although the movement recognised the Muslim Red Crescent. They reasoned that a proliferation of red symbols would detract from the original intention of the Red Cross emblem, which was to be a single emblem to mark vehicles and buildings protected on humanitarian grounds.

Certain Arab nations, such as Syria, also protested the entry of MDA into the Red Cross movement, making consensus impossible for a time. that was one of the most significant event in syria. However, from 2000 to 2006 the American Red Cross withheld its dues (a total of $42 million) to the International Federation of Red Cross and Red Crescent Societies (IFRC) because of IFRC's refusal to admit MDA; this ultimately led to the creation of the Red Crystal emblem and the admission of MDA on June 22, 2006.

The Red Star of David is not recognized as a protected symbol outside Israel; instead the MDA uses the Red Crystal emblem during international operations in order to ensure protection. Depending on the circumstances, it may place the Red Star of David inside the Red Crystal, or use the Red Crystal alone.

Criticism

The Australian TV network ABC and the indigenous rights group Friends of Peoples Close to Nature released a documentary called *Blood on the Cross* that raises allegations of the involvement of the Red Cross with the British military in conducting a massacre in the Southern Highlands of West Papua. Mark Davis investigates allegations about the role of the International Red Cross and the British military regarding the WWFWikipedia:Manual of Style hostages crisis, in May 1996. Following the broadcast of the documentary, the Red Cross announced publicly that it would appoint an individual outside the organization to investigate the allegations made in the film and any responsibility on its part. The report contends that it's not clear to which degree the Red Cross was involved, with some of the criticism concerning how well the organization handled the crisis.

Allegations of poor governance and concern over accountability and transparency within certain national societies have led to high profile resignations.

See also

- Accountable Fundraising
- Emblems of the International Red Cross and Red Crescent Movement
- International Committee of the Red Cross
- International Federation of Red Cross and Red Crescent Societies
- List of Red Cross and Red Crescent Societies
- Red Swastika Society
- logor Crveni Krst (Red Cross Camp)
- First Aid Convention Europe
- Roerich Pact

Further reading

Books

- David P. Forsythe: *Humanitarian Politics: The International Committee of the Red Cross.* Johns Hopkins University Press, Baltimore 1978, ISBN 0-8018-1983-0
- Henry Dunant: *A Memory of Solferino.* ICRC, Geneva 1986, ISBN 2-88145-006-7
- Jean-Claude Favez, *The Red Cross and the Holocaust*, Cambridge University Press 1999
- Hans Haug: *Humanity for all: the International Red Cross and Red Crescent Movement.* Henry Dunant Institute, Geneva in association with Paul Haupt Publishers, Bern 1993, ISBN 3-258-04719-7
- Georges Willemin, Roger Heacock: *International Organization and the Evolution of World Society. Volume 2: The International Committee of the Red Cross.* Martinus Nijhoff Publishers, Boston 1984, ISBN 90-247-3064-3
- Pierre Boissier: *History of the International Committee of the Red Cross. Volume I: From Solferino to Tsushima.* Henry Dunant Institute, Geneva 1985, ISBN 2-88044-012-2
- André Durand: *History of the International Committee of the Red Cross. Volume II: From Sarajevo to Hiroshima.* Henry Dunant Institute, Geneva 1984, ISBN 2-88044-009-2
- International Committee of the Red Cross: *Handbook of the International Red Cross and Red Crescent Movement.* 13th edition, ICRC, Geneva 1994, ISBN 2-88145-074-1
- John F. Hutchinson: *Champions of Charity: War and the Rise of the Red Cross.* Westview Press, Boulder 1997, ISBN 0-8133-3367-9
- Caroline Moorehead: *Dunant's dream: War, Switzerland and the history of the Red Cross.* HarperCollins, London 1998, ISBN 0-00-255141-1 (Hardcover edition); HarperCollins, London 1999, ISBN 0-00-638883-3 (Paperback edition)
- François Bugnion: *The International Committee of the Red Cross and the protection of war victims.* ICRC & Macmillan (ref. 0503), Geneva 2003, ISBN 0-333-74771-2
- Angela Bennett: *The Geneva Convention: The Hidden Origins of the Red Cross.* Sutton Publishing, Gloucestershire 2005, ISBN 0-7509-4147-2
- David P. Forsythe: *The Humanitarians. The International Committee of the Red Cross.* Cambridge University Press, Cambridge 2005, ISBN 0-521-61281-0

Journal articles

- François Bugnion: *The emblem of the Red Cross: a brief history.* ICRC (ref. 0316), Geneva 1977
- Jean-Philippe Lavoyer, Louis Maresca: *The Role of the ICRC in the Development of International Humanitarian Law.* In: *International Negotiation.* 4(3)/1999. Brill Academic Publishers, p. 503–527, ISSN 1382-340X

- Neville Wylie: *The Sound of Silence: The History of the International Committee of the Red Cross as Past and Present.* In: *Diplomacy and Statecraft.* 13(4)/2002. Routledge/ Taylor & Francis, p. 186–204, ISSN 0959-2296
- David P. Forsythe: "The International Committee of the Red Cross and International Humanitarian Law." In: *Humanitäres Völkerrecht - Informationsschriften. The Journal of International Law of Peace and Armed Conflict.* 2/2003, German Red Cross and Institute for International Law of Peace and Armed Conflict, p. 64–77, ISSN 0937-5414
- François Bugnion: *Towards a comprehensive Solution to the Question of the Emblem.* Revised 4th edition. ICRC (ref. 0778), Geneva 2006

External links

- International Red Cross and Red Crescent Movement [3] (magazine)
- Standing Commission of the Red Cross and Red Crescent [4]
- International Committee of the Red Cross (ICRC) [5]
- International Federation of Red Cross and Red Crescent Societies (IFRC) [6]
- Our world. Your move. (ICRC-IFRC) [7]
- Red Crescent and Red Cross Club [8]

Geographical coordinates: 46°13′40″N 6°8′14″E

Women's Land Army

Woman's Land Army of America

The **Woman's Land Army of America** (WLAA), later the **Women's Land Army** (WLA), was a civilian organization created during the First and Second World Wars to work in agriculture replacing men called up to the military. Women who worked for the WLAA were sometimes known as **farmerettes**. The WLAA was modeled on the British Women's Land Army.

First World War

The Woman's Land Army of America (WLAA) operated from 1917 to 1921, employing 15,000 - 20,000 urban women. Many were college educated, and units were associated with colleges. The WLAA was supported by Progressives like Teddy Roosevelt, and was strongest in the West and Northeast, where it was associated with the suffrage movement. Other groups helping to organize the WLAA included the Woman's National Farm and Garden Association (WNFGA), the Temple University Ambler staff, the State Council of Defense of some states, the Garden Club of America, and the YMCA. In addition to the WLAA, the U.S. government sponsored the U.S School Garden Army and the National War Garden Commission. Opposition came from Nativists, opponents of President Woodrow Wilson, and those who questioned the women's strength and the effect on their health.

World War II

The Women's Land Army (WLA) was formed as part of the United States Crop Corps, alongside the Victory Farm Volunteers (for teenage boys and girls), and lasted from 1943 to 1947. Almost 135,000 women were placed in Oregon alone. Other emergency farm worker programs in the U.S. included the Bracero Program (1942–1947), an agreement with Mexico.

See also

- Women's Land Army
- Australian Women's Land Army
- United States home front during World War II
- Victory garden
- Rosie the Riveter

Further reading

- Elaine F. Weiss (2008). *Fruits of Victory: The Woman's Land Army of America in the Great War.* ISBN 978-1-59797-273-4. (excerpts in *Smithsonian* [1]; NPR interview [2].)
- Stephanie A. Carpenter (2003). *On the Farm Front: The Women's Land Army in World War II.* ISBN 978-0875803142.
- "Agriculture [3]" in *The Great Plains During World War II*, ed. by R. Douglas Hurt. The Plains Humanities Alliance and the Center for Digital Research in the Humanities, University of Nebraska–Lincoln, 2008.

Article Sources and Contributors

Women's roles in the World Wars *Source*: http://en.wikipedia.org/?oldid=390598837 *Contributors*: Tide rolls

Greatest Generation *Source*: http://en.wikipedia.org/?oldid=389161104 *Contributors*: The Thing That Should Not Be

United States home front during World War II *Source*: http://en.wikipedia.org/?oldid=389789479 *Contributors*: Catgut

Women in the workforce *Source*: http://en.wikipedia.org/?oldid=389007381 *Contributors*: Lquilter

Rosie the Riveter *Source*: http://en.wikipedia.org/?oldid=389171318 *Contributors*: Clio2000

Willow Run Airport *Source*: http://en.wikipedia.org/?oldid=381243775 *Contributors*: 1 anonymous edits

Richmond Shipyards *Source*: http://en.wikipedia.org/?oldid=381056539 *Contributors*: Look2See1

Rosie the Riveter/World War II Home Front National Historical Park *Source*: http://en.wikipedia.org/?oldid=387903570 *Contributors*:

The Life and Times of Rosie the Riveter *Source*: http://en.wikipedia.org/?oldid=390388819 *Contributors*:

Women Airforce Service Pilots *Source*: http://en.wikipedia.org/?oldid=387727436 *Contributors*: Dave1185

United Service Organizations *Source*: http://en.wikipedia.org/?oldid=390436228 *Contributors*: Wikiwatcher1

International Red Cross and Red Crescent Movement *Source*: http://en.wikipedia.org/?oldid=390469997 *Contributors*: 1 anonymous edits

Woman's Land Army of America *Source*: http://en.wikipedia.org/?oldid=387725490 *Contributors*: Colfer2

Image Sources, Licenses and Contributors

Image:We Can Do It!.jpg *Source*: http://bibliocm.bibliolabs.com/mwAnon/index.php?title=File:We_Can_Do_It!.jpg *License*: unknown *Contributors*: -

Image:WWINavyYeoman1.jpg *Source*: http://bibliocm.bibliolabs.com/mwAnon/index.php?title=File:WWINavyYeoman1.jpg *License*: unknown *Contributors*: -

image:UK worker meets Roosevelt - Toni Frissell LC-F9-01-4211-92-2.jpg *Source*: http://bibliocm.bibliolabs.com/mwAnon/index.php?title=File:UK_worker_meets_Roosevelt_-_Toni_Frissell_LC-F9-01-4211-92-2.jpg *License*: unknown *Contributors*: -

Image:Female soldiers 1939.JPG *Source*: http://bibliocm.bibliolabs.com/mwAnon/index.php?title=File:Female_soldiers_1939.JPG *License*: unknown *Contributors*: -

Image:AlfredPalmerwelder1.jpg *Source*: http://bibliocm.bibliolabs.com/mwAnon/index.php?title=File:AlfredPalmerwelder1.jpg *License*: unknown *Contributors*: -

File:Synagogue D-Day3.jpg *Source*: http://bibliocm.bibliolabs.com/mwAnon/index.php?title=File:Synagogue_D-Day3.jpg *License*: unknown *Contributors*: -

Image:WomanFactory1940s.jpg *Source*: http://bibliocm.bibliolabs.com/mwAnon/index.php?title=File:WomanFactory1940s.jpg *License*: unknown *Contributors*: -

File:Riverting team2.jpg *Source*: http://bibliocm.bibliolabs.com/mwAnon/index.php?title=File:Riverting_team2.jpg *License*: unknown *Contributors*: -

Image:Wwii woman worker-edit.jpg *Source*: http://bibliocm.bibliolabs.com/mwAnon/index.php?title=File:Wwii_woman_worker-edit.jpg *License*: unknown *Contributors*: -

File:Military aircraft tires 1941.gif *Source*: http://bibliocm.bibliolabs.com/mwAnon/index.php?title=File:Military_aircraft_tires_1941.gif *License*: unknown *Contributors*: -

Image:Homefront posters.jpg *Source*: http://bibliocm.bibliolabs.com/mwAnon/index.php?title=File:Homefront_posters.jpg *License*: unknown *Contributors*: -

Image:Flying tigers pilot.jpg *Source*: http://bibliocm.bibliolabs.com/mwAnon/index.php?title=File:Flying_tigers_pilot.jpg *License*: unknown *Contributors*: Original uploader was Signaleer at en.wikipedia

Image:Portal-puzzle.svg *Source*: http://bibliocm.bibliolabs.com/mwAnon/index.php?title=File:Portal-puzzle.svg *License*: unknown *Contributors*: -

File:Richmond Shipyard No. 3 (Richmond, CA).jpg *Source*: http://bibliocm.bibliolabs.com/mwAnon/index.php?title=File:Richmond_Shipyard_No._3_(Richmond,_CA).jpg *License*: unknown *Contributors*: -

File:USA California location map.svg *Source*: http://bibliocm.bibliolabs.com/mwAnon/index.php?title=File:USA_California_location_map.svg *License*: unknown *Contributors*: -

File:Red pog.svg *Source*: http://bibliocm.bibliolabs.com/mwAnon/index.php?title=File:Red_pog.svg *License*: unknown *Contributors*: -

Image:PD-icon.svg *Source*: http://bibliocm.bibliolabs.com/mwAnon/index.php?title=File:PD-icon.svg *License*: unknown *Contributors*: -

File:We_Can_Do_It!.jpg *Source*: http://bibliocm.bibliolabs.com/mwAnon/index.php?title=File:We_Can_Do_It!.jpg *License*: unknown *Contributors*: -

Image:Richmond - Marina Bay - Rosie the Riveter monument 01.jpg *Source*: http://bibliocm.bibliolabs.com/mwAnon/index.php?title=File:Richmond_-_Marina_Bay_-_Rosie_the_Riveter_monument_01.jpg *License*: GNU Free Documentation License *Contributors*: Original uploader was Benefactor123 at en.wikipedia

Image:WWII daycare Richmond CA.jpg *Source*: http://bibliocm.bibliolabs.com/mwAnon/index.php?title=File:WWII_daycare_Richmond_CA.jpg *License*: unknown *Contributors*: -

File:NARA-542191-WASP-pilot.jpg *Source*: http://bibliocm.bibliolabs.com/mwAnon/index.php?title=File:NARA-542191-WASP-pilot.jpg *License*: unknown *Contributors*: -

File:400-202xtra.jpg *Source*: http://bibliocm.bibliolabs.com/mwAnon/index.php?title=File:400-202xtra.jpg *License*: unknown *Contributors*: -

File:020927-o-9999A-002.jpg *Source*: http://bibliocm.bibliolabs.com/mwAnon/index.php?title=File:020927-o-9999A-002.jpg *License*: unknown *Contributors*: -

File:Madge Moore WASP.JPG *Source*: http://bibliocm.bibliolabs.com/mwAnon/index.php?title=File:Madge_Moore_WASP.JPG *License*: unknown *Contributors*: -

File:WASP Congressional Gold Medal.jpg *Source*: http://bibliocm.bibliolabs.com/mwAnon/index.php?title=File:WASP_Congressional_Gold_Medal.jpg *License*: unknown *Contributors*: -

File:Jackiewasptrainees.jpg *Source*: http://bibliocm.bibliolabs.com/mwAnon/index.php?title=File:Jackiewasptrainees.jpg *License*: unknown *Contributors*: -

File:020927-o-9999A-003.jpg *Source*: http://bibliocm.bibliolabs.com/mwAnon/index.php?title=File:020927-o-9999A-003.jpg *License*: unknown *Contributors*: -

Image:Hope WWII 44.jpg *Source*: http://bibliocm.bibliolabs.com/mwAnon/index.php?title=File:Hope_WWII_44.jpg *License*: unknown *Contributors*: -

Image:Berlin-ship1944.jpg *Source*: http://bibliocm.bibliolabs.com/mwAnon/index.php?title=File:Berlin-ship1944.jpg *License*: Public Domain *Contributors*: US Govt.. Original uploader was Wikiwatcher1 at en.wikipedia

Image:USO Vietnam70.jpg *Source*: http://bibliocm.bibliolabs.com/mwAnon/index.php?title=File:USO_Vietnam70.jpg *License*: unknown *Contributors*: -

Image:Croixrouge logos.jpg *Source*: http://bibliocm.bibliolabs.com/mwAnon/index.php?title=File:Croixrouge_logos.jpg *License*: unknown *Contributors*: -

Image:Jean Henri Dunant.jpg *Source*: http://bibliocm.bibliolabs.com/mwAnon/index.php?title=File:Jean_Henri_Dunant.jpg *License*: unknown *Contributors*: -

Image:Original Geneva Conventions.jpg *Source*: http://bibliocm.bibliolabs.com/mwAnon/index.php?title=File:Original_Geneva_Conventions.jpg *License*: unknown *Contributors*: -

File:Flag of France.svg *Source*: http://bibliocm.bibliolabs.com/mwAnon/index.php?title=File:Flag_of_France.svg *License*: Public Domain *Contributors*: User:SKopp, User:SKopp, User:SKopp, User:SKopp, User:SKopp, User:SKopp

File:Flag of Hesse.svg *Source*: http://bibliocm.bibliolabs.com/mwAnon/index.php?title=File:Flag_of_Hesse.svg *License*: unknown *Contributors*: -

File:Flag of the Netherlands.svg *Source*: http://bibliocm.bibliolabs.com/mwAnon/index.php?title=File:Flag_of_the_Netherlands.svg *License*: unknown *Contributors*: -

File:Flag of Prussia (1803).gif *Source*: http://bibliocm.bibliolabs.com/mwAnon/index.php?title=File:Flag_of_Prussia_(1803).gif *License*: unknown *Contributors*: -

File:Romanov Flag.svg *Source*: http://bibliocm.bibliolabs.com/mwAnon/index.php?title=File:Romanov_Flag.svg *License*: unknown *Contributors*: -

File:Flag of Spain (1785-1873 and 1875-1931).svg *Source*: http://bibliocm.bibliolabs.com/mwAnon/index.php?title=File:Flag_of_Spain_(1785-1873_and_1875-1931).svg *License*: unknown *Contributors*: -

file:Honneur à la Croix-Rouge-1915.JPG *Source*: http://bibliocm.bibliolabs.com/mwAnon/index.php?title=File:Honneur_à_la_Croix-Rouge-1915.JPG *License*: unknown *Contributors*: -

file:Ernest Hemingway in Milan 1918 retouched 3.jpg *Source*: http://bibliocm.bibliolabs.com/mwAnon/index.php?title=File:Ernest_Hemingway_in_Milan_1918_retouched_3.jpg *License*: unknown *Contributors*: -

Image Sources, Licenses and Contributors

Image:HZwLazarecie1940.jpg *Source*: http://bibliocm.bibliolabs.com/mwAnon/index.php?title=File:HZwLazarecie1940.jpg *License*: unknown *Contributors*: -
Image:Marcel Junod-5.jpg *Source*: http://bibliocm.bibliolabs.com/mwAnon/index.php?title=File:Marcel_Junod-5.jpg *License*: unknown *Contributors*: -
Image:IKRK Hauptquartier.jpg *Source*: http://bibliocm.bibliolabs.com/mwAnon/index.php?title=File:IKRK_Hauptquartier.jpg *License*: unknown *Contributors*: -
Image:Henry Davison.jpg *Source*: http://bibliocm.bibliolabs.com/mwAnon/index.php?title=File:Henry_Davison.jpg *License*: unknown *Contributors*: -
Image:Friedensnobelpreis-1963.jpg *Source*: http://bibliocm.bibliolabs.com/mwAnon/index.php?title=File:Friedensnobelpreis-1963.jpg *License*: unknown *Contributors*: -
Image:Schweiz Genf IRK-Museum.jpg *Source*: http://bibliocm.bibliolabs.com/mwAnon/index.php?title=File:Schweiz_Genf_IRK-Museum.jpg *License*: unknown *Contributors*: -
Image:Emblem of the ICRC.svg *Source*: http://bibliocm.bibliolabs.com/mwAnon/index.php?title=File:Emblem_of_the_ICRC.svg *License*: unknown *Contributors*: -
Image:Emblem of the IFRC.svg *Source*: http://bibliocm.bibliolabs.com/mwAnon/index.php?title=File:Emblem_of_the_IFRC.svg *License*: unknown *Contributors*: -
Image:Flag of the Red Cross.svg *Source*: http://bibliocm.bibliolabs.com/mwAnon/index.php?title=File:Flag_of_the_Red_Cross.svg *License*: unknown *Contributors*: -
Image:Flag of Switzerland.svg *Source*: http://bibliocm.bibliolabs.com/mwAnon/index.php?title=File:Flag_of_Switzerland.svg *License*: unknown *Contributors*: -
Image:Flag of the Red Crescent.svg *Source*: http://bibliocm.bibliolabs.com/mwAnon/index.php?title=File:Flag_of_the_Red_Crescent.svg *License*: unknown *Contributors*: -
Image:Flag of the Red Crystal.svg *Source*: http://bibliocm.bibliolabs.com/mwAnon/index.php?title=File:Flag_of_the_Red_Crystal.svg *License*: unknown *Contributors*: -
Image:Red Lion with Sun.svg *Source*: http://bibliocm.bibliolabs.com/mwAnon/index.php?title=File:Red_Lion_with_Sun.svg *License*: unknown *Contributors*: -
Image:Red Star of David.svg *Source*: http://bibliocm.bibliolabs.com/mwAnon/index.php?title=File:Red_Star_of_David.svg *License*: unknown *Contributors*: -
File:13492v.jpg *Source*: http://bibliocm.bibliolabs.com/mwAnon/index.php?title=File:13492v.jpg *License*: unknown *Contributors*: -

The cover image herein is used under a Creative Commons License and may be reused or reproduced under that same license.

http://upload.wikimedia.org/wikipedia/commons/1/1a/WomanFactory1940s.jpg

CPSIA information can be obtained at www.ICGtesting.com
Printed in the USA
LVOW131920070212

267543LV00012B/103/P